The SISTER CHRONICLES
*
AND OTHER POEMS

By Joyce Nower

The Sister Chronicles and Other Poems

iUniverse books may be ordered through booksellers or by contacting:

*iUniverse
1663 Liberty Drive
Bloomington, IN 47403
www.iuniverse.com
1-800-Authors (1-800-288-4677)*

*Because of the dynamic nature of the Internet, any web addresses or links
contained in this book may have changed since publication and may no longer be
valid. The views expressed in this work are solely those of the author and do not
necessarily reflect the views of the publisher, and the publisher hereby disclaims
any responsibility for them.*

*ISBN: 978-1-4697-3872-7 (sc)
ISBN: 978-1-4697-3873-4 (e)
ISBN: 978-1-4697-3874-1 (dj)*

Library of Congress Control Number: 2012902028

Printed in the United States of America

iUniverse rev. date: 2/10/2012

The SISTER CHRONICLES

AND OTHER POEMS

By Joyce Nower

Edited and with a Foreword by
Leon Nower

FOR LEON, AGAIN and AGAIN

CONTENTS

PART IV. THE SISTER CHRONICLES

PART V. MT. HELIX SONGS

PART VI. SAILING AWAY

ACKNOWLEDGMENTS

Thanks to the editors of the magazines in which the following poems appeared, sometimes in different versions:

Anderbo: "Crow's Fault"
Andwerv: "Alone in the Desert"
Avatar Review: "On the Roof," "The Back Yard"
California Quarterly: "The Village"
Crescent Moon Journal: "The Lot Next Door" (Honorable Mention)
Eden Waters Press: The Home Anthology, "Humble Skills"; The Journey Anthology, "Sailing Away," "Triptych," "Where Judgment Bobs and Weaves"
Feile-Festa: "Pop"
Kaleidowhirl Literary Journal: "There Was a Time"
Letters to the World: "Maybe the Rocks Did Soften in the Sun"
Poemeleon: "The Bridge of Sighs"
Psychological Perspectives: "Willows and Grasses"
The LBJ: "The Wrentit"
The 2008 San Diego Poetry Annual: "The Wild Parrots"
Umbrella: "Tomatoes and Tomato Cages"
Visions-International: "Fishing with Bamboo Pole," "At the End of the Road"
Worm 38: "More Like Athene Than the Willendorf Venus"

EDITOR'S ACKNOWLEDGMENTS

I wish to thank Melissa Hughes for her generous and priceless help in designing and preparing this book for publication, Minh Nguyen for sharing the beautiful photo that introduces Part V, the eagle-eyed Mark Troedson for proofreading the manuscript, Colette Nower and Lisa Hoffman for useful suggestions and, of course, the excellent staff of iUniverse who guided the entire process of publication.

Leon Nower

FORWARD

The nineteen-sixties and -seventies were years of great turmoil and change in our country. Behind the purple haze of loosening lifestyles, great political and personal struggles were being waged. Dominant among them was the anti-war movement and what one might call the empowerment struggles, including the quest for civil and human rights — spanning the spectrum from Martin Luther King, Jr. and Cesar Chavez to Malcolm X and the Black Panthers — educational reform, and the all-encompassing Women's Movement.

Joyce Nower (1932-2010) was a passionate participant and leader in most of these outcries for a better world. Most importantly, she was a co-founder of the first Women's Studies Department in the United States, and perhaps the world, at San Diego State University in 1970. "Sister Chronicles," the title poem which constitutes Part IV of this book, is actually a series of poems that deal with this momentous event in the history of women's struggles for equal rights.

The sailing, however, was anything but smooth. One would have expected the tragi-comic opposition by the older conservative faculty — thankfully, two vice-presidents and two deans proved sympathetic and helpful — but what hurt were the strident attacks and accusations (a friend referred to them as intra-movement cannibalism) by "sisters" from the left, who yelled "sellouts," "cooptation," "elitism," and so on, their rhetoric sadly similar to that of the Reign of Terror which accompanied the French Revolution. At one point they even succeeded in taking over the department and almost ran it into the ground before a competent scholar was hired to chair and rebuild the department.

It all started when Joyce, a San Diego State instructor, met a student activist, Carol Rowell (now Council). They had both been engaged in a variety of activities but realized after a few conversations that, somehow, feminism had always been kept in the background. They convened a "consciousness-raising rap group" composed of students plus Joyce. After much painful sharing of personal experiences with sexism — at home, at school, in society in general, and even within the progressive movements they were a part of — someone said, "OK, my consciousness has been raised enough for now, and I am tired of belly-aching! What do we do?" They proceeded to give substance to the feminist dictum: "The Personal Is Political."

They came up with the then novel idea of a women's center that would meet the personal, educational, cultural and employment needs of women that were not adequately, if at all, provided for by our patriarchal society. Being part of the academy, they conceived of a center that would straddle the campus and the community. They named it the Center for Women's Studies and Services (CWSS) and used their contacts, on and off campus, to procure seed funds for the project. They divided the Center into functional units they called "components": a Storefront in downtown San Diego to help women with employment and training; a Cultural Component that, among other things, mounted an annual Women's Arts Festival across five floors of the Love library and brought in artists from around the country; a Publications Component that published a nationally distributed newspaper, "The Longest Revolution," as well as, under Joyce's editorship, one of the first anthologies of women's poetry; a Counseling Component that developed innovative feminist counseling and provided an "Underground Railroad" for women who needed to get away from violent husbands or boyfriends, and set up Sisterhood Chapters in women's correctional institutions and on other campuses; and finally, the Education Component dedicated, among other educational endeavors, to establishing a Women's Studies department at SDSU (see pp 75-115, esp. pp 103 on).

When asked to describe her "poetic voice," Joyce said that in each poem she strove to find the voice and technique appropriate to the poem, thus giving the subject matter primacy over form. She was fond of the comment by George Bernard Shaw that "art for art's sake" was a luxury of the privileged. Thus, you will find in this volume couplets as well as free verse, sonnets as well as a mix of prose and poetry, as is the case in Part IV. The latter technique — although it seemed strange to some early readers of the poem — goes at least as far back as Dante's "La Vita Nuova" and, more recently, the work of the poet H.D.

Part IV is clearly the heart of the book. Parts I, II, and III give us the social, political, historic and personal background that led to Joyce's passionate commitment to progressive change in these four dimensions of the human saga. They reveal without any self-consciousness her deep scholarship as well as her talent for bringing together effortlessly relevant insights from antiquity to the present age.

The final two parts are a deep sigh after a great effort, a "Good Bye to All That." They are a return to her other passions: nature, family, beauty, writing, teaching, and martial arts. They speak for themselves.

JERICHO AGAIN
AND AGAIN

*"The man who never alters his opinion is like standing water, and breeds reptiles of the mind." – **Blake***

1. The Psychic Status Quo

Go to any city and you'll find
the conquered, immigrants, the down and outs,

the poor, the rich, the homeless on the ramps,
in fact, the way it is, and in the mind,

its rough draft, a way to feel, to see,
to be, a psychic status quo set up

by border streets and chain link fence, a free-
way cutting through, a railroad track —

fixed mind unable to shake loose of it,
even if it sees its opposite,

hard put to shift gears in one short life,
where justice isn't often politic,

where justice never is just at the start,
but, if at all, at the end, quixotic

bursts of splendid snatches of song at least,
the piper weaving in and out among

the clink of glasses, raucous laughter, chat,
the notes hard to hear above the feast.

2. The Gold Spoon, the Taste of Dust

Or say a town springs up close by a stream
bending seaward, or on land once dense

with oak or birch or elm. If it becomes
a traveled crossroads and then is fenced

off in sections based on this trade, that skill,
the flats and hills where haves and have-nots live

(often the gold spoon, the taste of dust,
no matter character or wit or will)

will stand as right in unreflective mind.
That's the way it is. After all,

CEO's, judges, kings, presidents,
signal for day to start, for night to fall,

for tanks to roll, and guns be raised, to tout
the panoplies of power, the rest of us

placed here for them, (you and me — the rout,
the silent rabble), servicing the schemes

of power, asleep, until a new will dreams
a newer song, notes dim above the din.

3. Alexandria, Egypt (3-4 A.D.)

Hypatia's city looked like mine, it seems,
 with palms of beaded gold where beehives hide,

a curving harbor sluiced by flickering light,
trade and pleasure craft, warships, triremes.

Alexandria's broad and well-lit avenues
split it into quarters. One for Greek

elite. One (before the purge) for Jews.
Rhacotis for Egyptians in the west.

The fourth — Negro, Arab, Persian, Syrian —
the "flammable welter" of the Mediterranean.

Outside the city wall, a sister polis
of burial mounds where great and small shared

sacred silent space. But in her classes,
Christian, Pagan, Jew, Manichaean, mystic,

Arab, Roman, Greek, Egyptian, Afric —
mix of the Great Sea, albeit elite —

entered together the Eden of the mind,
their music playing to a different time.

4. Great Neck, Long Island, New York (1945-1949)

And in Great Neck, the Old Village — Polish,
Irish, Catholic — kept to itself with no cause

to believe pre-World War II that post-war
interfaith meetings would please the Lord.

And in the New Village, second generation
English, Swiss, and French, Germans, too,

mowed their lawns — Unitarians, Episcopalians,
Congregationalists. Then urban Jews,

prewar, became postwar suburbanites,
and refugees ("right off the boat") moved on

the Island fleeing camps ten years too late,
ready, (the synagogue, a halfway site

between the Old and New), eager to meet
with Protestants, and when the Catholic

God from the Burning Bush to the Bishopric
said yes, with them. A muster of citizens,

they attacked the shadows in the mind
and tried to heal the divisions of that time.

5. San Diego, California (Before 1960)

Again, consider that in San Diego
before the commerce of Mission Valley, a trail

of missions led back to a tale of Cibola,
the seventh city, with gold roof tiles, a trail

that dead ends on the harbor's western crown
of sycamore, summer home to the tribe-

of-eight-homes, and in the eastern hills at live
oak groves where acorns fall on fall's high ground,

where lilac splash the rise, and wildcats bound.
That mix of Portuguese and Spanish and slaves,

the western push of Eastern whites — raids,
rails, round-ups, is History's shooting match.

Mexican, Anglo, before the frontier fades,
mingle for a moment, then decline

to language lines, "like drawn to like," packed
later into color's unspoken code.

Homegrown segregation — San Diego mode.
The Ebony Motel — our artifact.

6. San Diego, California (1960's-1980's)

Reservations for us all, so to speak:
North County, rich white. Asians, off I-5.

Blacks, Chicanos, routed to Southeast.
Yes, a Lincoln High. And white police

recruited from the South. (Until the Sixties,
no Blacks walked north of Broadway downtown!)

Out East County — trucks and gun racks — where good
ole boys hung out. The melting pot ground down

in Golden Hill beneath the heel of dealers.
Brandish a few statistics (Pillipinas

commit suicide in greatest numbers),
witness ways of self-preservation (Chaldeans

in the mom-and-pop's wear large gold crosses),
yet truth be told the blonde beast freely runs,

and physiology, the gene pool, and brains
(Dr. Van Evrey: African nerve ends

less sensitive to the whip) still are sources
of argument, "scientific" and "closely reasoned."

7. Childhood's Globe of Light

The china cat and kittens smugly sit
among the atomizers and survey

a world of light pink walls and ruffled drapes
and with a steady feline gaze they stay

each object in its proper place. Their power
ends at the edge of books jammed on the shelf,

at the green glass buoy that floated in from fisher
nets and washed up on Peconic shores.

There is another side to the yellow moon
which only I knew as I hurried to my room.

Now it comes in polar light, drenched,
like icecaps melting, latitude longitude

snapped, swift peace in the eyes, the wrenched
heart dazzled into love. This was not God,

but prowling the great bone arch of the body's form,
seeing the ode of the body's solo song,

and outside the ring of light, my straight-backed chair,
my jeans and rumpled shirt, my long brown hair.

8. Childhood's "Once Upon a Time"

"Once upon a time" — those magic words
weave fact and fantasy on childhood's loom —

at cock's crow in the City of the Moon,
striped tents and golden turrets rose to greet

the Princess of the Moon bade soon to sleep.
With her, an entourage of varied girth

and hue now gathered from the ends of earth.
A stew of teeth and eyes and noses — flat,

up-turned and bulbous. Legs both thin and fat.
Hair braided, frizzed, in spikes or corn rows, turbaned.

Rigged out in silken capes and blouses trimmed
in peacock feathers. Heavy the morning heat,

the shining air, heavy their eyes with sleep.
Companions led companions into dream

in the safety of a state in which, I dreamed,
politics was trust and will, not lies

or ruinous policies or payoffs, wrongs
to make life brutish, cheap, and long.

9. Realities

The City of the Moon exists in lore:
But here the ruins of Will fan out and day

turns shrill and night hides writing on the wall.
The fields where yesterday cows grazed are mall

and hotel high-rise, and the boy-next-door
now deals in drugs. Even on sunny days

someone beats his wife, skinheads scrawl
slurs, and mountain meadows reboot

as trailer parks. Drifts of silver foil
push up against the eucalyptus root

on freeway ramps, and trees turn dry and brown
and stand like dead men in a burned out town,

victims of a scorched earth policy.
Hopeless at its dark core the city dies,

not intimate with nature — the violet hue
of autumn light, the seas, the open skies

(horizon's call to high adventure and dream) —
what we came out of and what we go to.

10. Faith

Faith comes mysterious: a picture from
a child's book, a natural fact, a dream.

One can smell outposts of black sage,
see snake cholla on canyon cliffs between

highways or in Pacific waters surf
off a silver strip of river silt spit out

by southwesters, hike down streams of dust
that once rinsed deltas, flashed chub and trout.

Deer trod these golden hills, wildcat, bear,
and antelope. Just yesterday, towhee

and jay, rising like a bursting flare
tossed on a hot breeze from the bay, signaled

that somewhere in the back country in low
scrub oak and toyon bush and mountain lilac,

in some secret natural room sunbursts
and lizards light up walls of stone. I track

my way to longings beyond the trance
of tribe, into the votive mind's expanse.

11. Hope

A poet said the city of the just
lies inside the unjust city: hope

lies in that. Each time, change, we trust,
will harden into less cruel rebirths,

like no arm into a broken arm. We hope
(against hope often) for daily life to rove

past boundaries. In school, at work, men
and women meet in wildlife corridors of

the heart and make a life of boundaries
defunct, that life a cheerless minimalism,

monochrome, like calling "music" one stone
on another. Our music pipes a rhythm

remaking myth: Say the languorous snake,
its great coils spiraling down around the trunk,

lying in wait, the darting small sleek head
a flick away from Eve, its patience great,

its pretty voice oiled, lies in wait
to pounce and gulp — make it sway instead.

12. Charity

If boundaries don't naturally erode,
and social will needs forging, then the search

is on for friends who speak unspoken words
(between parentheses), and then out loud.

Step by step, we scheme a strategy,
let loose subversion to help history,

set forth tactics, recruit, distribute chores,
"Abandon Hope, Yet Hope," our philosophy.

One last metaphor: If there's a town
that needs re-vision and we are gathered there,

hands clasped, the motley circle vibrant, grown
— may love give birth to love, not hate or fear! —

and we start to dance around that city wall
describing a new iconography of will

beneath the sky, and should each step rebound
a shout, and if there are enough of us,

those shouts, that strange dance, and that mass
will blast that wall and bring that city down.

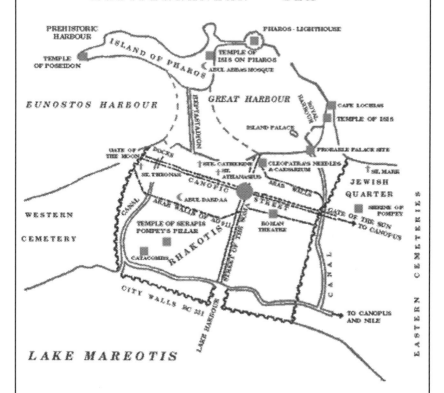

MEDITATIONS ON HYPATIA OF ALEXANDRIA

Hypatia *was a mathematician-philosopher and mystic who lived and worked in Alexandria and was renowned throughout the ancient world. The most recent plausible dates for her are 355 A.D. — 415 A.D. Bishop Cyril, later sainted by the Church, preached jeremiads against her, probably inciting the mob of fanatical monks who murdered and dismembered her on a church altar.*

1. A Wintry Blast in the Ear of Saint Cyril

Hypatia, churches make mistakes, but asked
to confess — no way. Once Evil's blessed,
forget redress, so, Saint(ly) Cyril, lest
your sleep's too sweet, here's a wintry blast
in your ear or any other orifice.
Wiping pagans out was your blood sport
& what you left winds up a short report:
Hypatia. Thinker. Scientist crossed
with mystic. Scraps of life unearthed
in bios, tracts, notes from Synesius
(who wrestled with the resurrection thesis).
So let me briefly resurrect your worth,
Hypatia, blowing siroccos of heated words
across dogmatic, theocratic graves.

2. The Eleventh Commandment
(One More for St. Cyril)

Let's get it straight. Not all saints are holy
but serve some bureaucratic function first:
lobotomize freethinkers, schismatics curse,
chop up the pagans. Whatever the policy
each institution breeds its own enforcer
and sainted Cyril was IT, a first class shit.
In a city where the polity was split,
he goaded gangs of desert monks to murder,
walk lockstep in the streets, destroy the temple.
Roused Peter the Reader, scribe, to forcefeed
God an Eleventh Commandment: Thou Shalt Bleed.
One was hand; the other, brain. Simple
justice subverts the immunity of time —
condemned, both, in the trial of my mind.

3. Scales Can't Calculate*

Hypatia, Math, God One, can't plot the locus
of soul and star, predict exactly where
and when you die, whose hand deals death. No hocus
pocus by priests decodes the vicious stare
of wilding in the streets, can tell you what
your agony (dismemberment), who scooped
up bones laid on the altar cloth, a clot
where life had been, for sixty years about.
Aghast, I piece the broken tale together —
that's all that's left — but shards don't make a cup.
And giving what? Not solace. Still I wonder
why era after era the step up
is so worn down, why scales can't calculate
malaise, the depth of lack, the height of hate.

A note on the word "wilding": "Wilding" is a word coined in the 1990's to describe gang violence against solitary women walking or jogging in Central Park, New York City.

4. Fast Forward 2K Years

Your stay in Athens turned you off: just word
games, bones, and charms — no scientific leaven.
As well you didn't swim with me — fast forward
about 2K years — in that effulgent heaven
Aegean, drenched in myth past the horizon.
A crystal universe! I swam off shore,
alone, first walking over round black stone
that quickly dropped off into metaphor:
"Swimming in the sky!" Swimming "foam-
flecked seas" that floated the Persian fleet, the Greek
triremes! To swim to where the sun now steeps
in sea, to see the gods amass, hear speech
refreshed, in meaning rich before it staled,
to float forever dazzled on their world!

5. Waste in the Chalices of the Dead

Your sadness wasn't that you left Athens,
or that rough seas purged you of its magic
nor was it, on your arrival, Father Theon's
news that squads of marauding monks, hand-picked,
desert-spawned, black cloaks with cedar stick
and knife, attacked the temple and its defenders,
scholars, many not worshipers, yet civic
souls, peaceful, law-abiding teachers,
but that the desecration seemed so complete:
monks camped at the foot of the god, offering bowls
used for food, and waste in the chalices of the dead,
and the last open words of pagan thought spread
out in the dirt, as before a scythe in wheat,
grain, or meteor showers in August heat.

6. Not Your Cup of Tea

Romantic love was not your cup of tea.
According to Damascius, you showed
a student with a crush on you your bloody
rag. The message: shake off the body's hold!
While standing in a market checkout lane,
I can see other rags, pulp, that track
down A and B, and A & what's-her-name.
And C. A tawdry sludge of mix and match.
No wonder that you focused on the mind,
and not as courtesan to thought, but thought
itself, in you, its festive breadth, its climb
towards peaks beyond itself, itself a thought
that comes and goes. Breathtaking the route!
Heavy breathing was no substitute.

7. Biology a Kind of Destiny

Flaccid, passive, slouched — one way to go.
Another, hardened hands to drive in nails.
Endurance trained into a runner's flow.
Or Isadora, eloquent in veils.
Biology — a kind of destiny.
Not just the egg and sperm of it, but coin
of being: bone and muscle's legacy,
the violin vibrato in the groin.
Transcend all this? But why? This miracle!
The most ascetic Self should take time off
if licked by lust — that flame that melts the mettle
of the mind into springtime stuff —
so like a famished bear come out to feast,
should hunker down, prepared to eat and eat.

8. Gold

(Thinking about Hypatia, my gold bracelet from Apartheid South Africa, and a New York Times article by David Sanger, headlined "Nazi Gold Was Recast and Issued the U.S.")

Gold outlines fantasy — the cockerel, egg,
the pot of, treasure buried under eaves,
but in apartheid my gold charm was dug,
and your gold oars in Sumion by slaves,
and blocks of gold once looted from the Dutch —
a backwards transmutation — mixed with gold
from teeth, from watches, rings, Grandma's brooch —
(Swiss banks, the neutral middleman) were sold
on global markets, & — surprise! — the Federal
vaults, swastikas off, mutated it,
Manhattan's stash, to post-war collateral —
blood into bonds! — for Spain and ITT.
(New York! "The sidewalks of!" "The light fantastic!"
The Met! Grand Central! El Greco at the Frick!)

9. Cities of the Dead

The City of the Dead in Brooklyn, a compound
of god-fearing Germans (no French or Jews,
Aunt said, foreseeing socials underground),
ignores at this late date a world view.
Outside your city wall your cemetery,
a sister city where burial mounds of great
and humble, in clay and marble symmetry,
held bones rotting at different rates.
Was it laid out like the city in four quarters:
the eastern - Jews; northwest, for the Egyptians;
the posh and well-lit, Greeks? Then, "Whatevers" —
Negro, Arab, Persian, Anatolians.
Your school: a mix of this and that, a still
reflection of you, the locus of good will.

10. Questions for a Neo-Platonist

You didn't dis the gods, you just dismissed
their nibs, (age twelve I staged a strike, refused
to dress for church — for sixty years I've missed
my ride), were called a heretic, accused
of seeing clearly through the veil just One.
What turned you off? That sculpture of Serapis
where priests on ladders used a megaphone?
A God who sternly vetoed pork and goddess?
Church dogma that sacked temples, gave the sign
to monks to cruise the streets with clubs? Or magic —
the future in intestines, charms, red wine
to blood? Like walking through a mine field. Say it:
All that we have is the folding and unfolding,
our own unceasing resonance embracing.

11. There Was a Time

There was a time the thought of many gods
pleased me more than did the thought of none.
In foam flakes curled over green Peconic waves
I sought Her eyes, and above the curved horizon,
if I held my eyes just so, an outline of hip
and thigh straddled the bulwark of shoreline rocks.
And when in a back-creek quiet, I stopped to dip
my hand, I heard His voice in soft sucks
of water lapping at mussels and reeds. Not
one doubt who was thunder. In St. Paul's,
kneeling on the worn-down altar step
where God appears in wine and wafer, all
I'm sure I heard was a gliss of girlish laughter
thrilling the lilies on the Easter altar.

12. Éclairs Are Better

That ass Palladas (squeaky voice well suited
to his petty poems) slips them out
his sleeve at every chance (even grabbed
the megaphone to greet you on the dock!)
I think he has a point: better to bore
your friends with a mulch of words that might sprout
metaphors (however strained) and hope for
a third or fourth or fifth noun to take root
(even though conjunctive adverbs thrive
and adjectives puff up like cream éclairs)
than squander them on strangers who arrive
in some cafe to sit on folding chairs
balancing a latté and a degree
in Creative Writing — genre: poetry.

13. More Like Athene Than the Willendorf Venus

That's us? That series of knobs, that blob of hip,
that hanging gut, freckled with dugs, no,
not a Barbie, a dyspeptic anorexic,
but more like a bozo rolling to and fro.
Good god! How get through the day with a chassis
that moves like squid at the ATM, to pitch
it over when you drop a dime, to mass it
when you tie a lace! And to scratch an itch!
Not a swimmer like you and me (eons
ago), at ease in a girl's body breaking through
waves, feet kicking foam, rangy arms
paddles, the body a keel cutting through.
My choice, Athene, struck on a Greek medallion,
greaves and all, one foot on the neck of a lion.

14. Friction Cranks Out Factions

Mistake: you can't be neutral in a skirt
(fast forward to the Sixties: jeans and shirt),
and friction cranks out factions, ready-made,
one group one up, another, retrograde.
Patriarch and Prefect warred on each other.
Serapis was torn down by monk marauders.
Trade turned to envy: synagogues burned down.
Churches rose up. "Idols" strewed the ground.
(In our decade, the Movement had'em all —
hipsters, SWPers, RSU, cultural
separatists, and Just Plain Mean.) Mystic?
Aloof and female? Witch! Separate
church and state? A clear unholy feint
to turn a saint to sinner, a sinner to saint!

15. Arise!

Pure blood? The final fascist fantasy,
mind's box within a box, the barbed wire gate.
Or, a twist, genocide through rape.
There is a timeless zest to brutality.
But we are baptized in the sluice of time
that spills love and hate over the land
to ebb and flow in man and woman,
dissolving custom in its wavy line.
It mixes us, through diaspora, trade,
invasion, mixed the Great Sea Christian, pagan,
Jew, African, Greek, Egyptian,
its aureole a shimmer even in shade,
and here, where Vietnamese, Somalis, Thais,
and more rise upwards on the flood. Arise!

16. History Is the Strangest Bird

Life preens its feathers, chirps its birthday songs,
while Death on wild wings swoops down and hovers.
History is the strangest bird. It's summer's
crow that caws through saw-toothed palm tree fronds,
a wary eye dissecting peace and war,
mine strikes, oil crises, deals, the smoke-filled room.
The rondo danced across a catacomb
of corpses, stacked beneath earth's dancing floor.
Gouged, raped, hammered, hung, dismembered,
bled, boiled, quartered, knifed, or brained —
the participles swell the rank terrain,
all abstract, who's who not quite remembered.
Down here rise cypress like candles on a cake.
From up there, they look like mourners at a wake.

17. Me and Celtic Bui[*]
(In honor of the Celtic Nun of Beare)

Of all the wonders, Stonehenge, Empire State,
Sumion where winds blow thick with strife
from war dead hammering the rocky cape,
age may subtract the greatest — daily life.
Like Celtic Bui will I shiver in sun and moan
as wind dies in the trees? Day and night
the body's bones feel more at home with stone
and mountain scrub than gardens of delight.
Too soon the couplet lengthens to lament,
the march slows to recessional, and mirth
once gone is gone. Peevishly extend
the lease on failing eyes and rotten teeth?
No landlord, Fool. Just Ebb-Tide-on-the-Shore!
And monthly dues in dunes of metaphor!

*Celtic Bui, or the Nun of Beare, or the Old Woman of Beare,
Ireland, may be an ancient earth-figure, or simply an old woman.*

18. A Pillbox Hat and a Hydroscope

It all comes down to keepsakes and memories,
once private, now glassed in the auction gallery
of, say, Christie's: like a pillbox hat— Jackie's,
or Dietrich's gift from Noel, a cane, ebony.
At yours, if you had one, wonders for sale:
a hydroscope, designed to measure liquids
(medicine when you had a cold — Cyril
branded it "unholy"), lectures on conics,
meditations on Plotinus, braille
tablets used at St. Didymus' School.
Me, I didn't wait for death. Those frail
sisters (my poems), hauling Nature and Soul
to Goodwill, are probably shelved in between
a book on nerves and a bio of Steve McQueen.

19. Never a Sixty Plus-Year-Old-Murdered Muse

You loved the city that did you in, its docks
stacked with wine and grain, its streets in grids,
the citizens, like your students, a polyglot.
The women, in the marketplace, at feasts,
out and about. You grew older and wiser
there, as famous as it, but myths make use
of youth and beauty, none past menses, never
a sixty plus-year-old-murdered Muse.
Flip through Bulfinch, The Age of (Male) Fable —
Helen's a whelp, the Danaïdes, girl brides,
Medea, a scary mom. Sure, the Pythian oracle
is old. Like Hecuba, dried up as herbs.
But your myth required youth, through the glass
of robes and tweeds, pipes, beards, moustache.

20. Death's Stony Presence

Each night the city of the living turns
into a sleeping city, a mimic
of death's stony presence. Flesh relearns
its fate and bites the dust. A small trick.
Like buildings viewed as tombstone monoliths.
And how to figure out this ruthless cycle?
Is our strangeness eased by seeing "life's
design" in everything— a Grand Total?
Why should Death core us, then unwind
words to stitch our body bag? Absurd!
As if no empty pages stirred behind
the ones with words. Strange, to love the Word,
to live and die by it, always unwinding —
One, God, Being, Unity, Nothing.

SOUNDINGS

1. At the End of the Road

At the end of the road a woods where patches of moss
greened the north side of trees and jack-in-the-pulpit
and violets flowered the hollows of downed trunks.

A stream like a child dreaming, arms and legs
akimbo, sprawled across black leaves and knotted
roots. Looking up, the trees hung down from the sky.

Dusk is the pillow where daylight naps, and syllables
of childhood have time to stutter into words.
Who enters returns a convert to herself.

By the time it was all cut down, reduced to houses,
a border had been drawn between me
and the eaves over the lengthening asphalt road.

2. Two Chews on Onion Grass

Two chews on onion grass picked near the pond
across the street — my exotic taste satisfied.
Each spring clumps reappeared like the pond itself.

Tadpoles, dragonflies, fairy shrimp.
Water eddied around a stem and a stem
stirred the water like a finger. Swift life.

Potent ephemera. Energy hatched within
birth, origin buried into substance
under shells and cuticles to resist desiccation.

If it can. What triggers in substrate by a shift
in weather. Hope. Even though turtles scavenge
salamander eggs, wood frogs croak each night.

3. Two Rings

Two rings. The sanctus bell called us to kneel
and benediction spilled through the vaulted nave.
I longed for a miracle, as if chant alone could conjure,

or sun, flaring through stained glass robes, thicken
the air with presence, as it layered red on gold.
Even sprawled under dogwood, I waited impatient,

as clouds rafting a glowering sky massed
in a bank of expectation, then finally burst
into shimmering ribbons. Indisputable sanctions

for the urgent globe of light that formed one day
between my hands. Inside was outside. The line
between body and mind snapped. All of it soul.

4. The Lot Next Door

We weathered changes in the lot next door.
Wet-kneed, intent, we crouched, solitary
conscripts, smoothing cracks in snow fort walls.

Through the monastic hush of trees, white gleamed,
then burst into a salvo of snowballs that shook
the branches bare. Spring meltdown swelled the trees

and from the thatch of maples, rope vines swung
us trunk to trunk. On summer nights our shadows
trapped lightning bugs in sparkling jelly jars,

and set them free when Mother called us in.
Winter, spring, summer, again and again.
Until no one called us, and the season passed.

5. Willows and Grasses

Willows and grasses rake the dark pond.
Knee deep in silence, I watch the ripples
of a water snake pirouette towards me

in the fulgent continuum of childhood that shades
into the somber end of summer twilight
filling up the stand of maples in the lot

next door, while lightning bugs move sedately
in and out. No hierarchies. No hatreds.
Being is the meditation, as simple

as a girl breaking through waves, feet kicking
up foam, arms rotating paddles brown
and strong, the body a keel cutting through.

6. Humble Skills

Humble skills. Patience polished into
learned naturalness, practiced hands cupped
catching water from the bathroom tap.

Small fingers finally formed a sealed hollow,
a pool to reflect an eye to see one day
sky well up over rock and water, a system.

Years later, biking near a Vermont town,
I stopped by icy pools of water formed
in polished rock like rounded bowls worn down

by endless invisible streams that slaked the thirst
of sycamores and pines ranging the mountains.
I knelt down and cupped my hands to drink.

7. Dead Shot

Dead shot? Still I performed the childhood rites.
Brush off cement. Knees on the line. Hands
a body-width away. I held the marble

between thumb and index finger, readied the right
palm heel, and let it hover like a hawk.
My eyes locked on my victims — puries, cat

eyes, aggies, steelies, biggies — bug-eyed rabbits
lined up six feet away. Only the Shooter
swirled in its fixed orbit — from eye to brain

to arm to hand to target. Muscles snapped to.
For the first and last time Chance was not a partner.
Life clicked in to the thrill of immutable law.

8. Hoops

We listened for the tapping of her cane,
then her dragging foot, as she labored
down the corridor past study hall to gym,

as if repetition would make each step perfect.
Her limp bounced brightly off high walls
until a crutch replaced the cane, then two,

and the dragging sound followed a longer pause
and the silences between were more profound.
Coach took us along with her, at least part way,

into a world where even though we jumped
through hoops, we didn't always win the game,
no matter clean uniforms, straight lines, straight backs.

9. World War II's Queen of Scrap

A victory garden of scrap. Bedsteads. Tin cans.
Rusted tools. A broken flashlight. Rims.
I scavenged scrap in alleys, and dragged it home.

The apple tree presided, that same tree
I sat in for hours, now from roots a metal
welt rising. Then carted off and crushed.

Melted down. For what — guns? Canteens?
Stock years later in army surplus stores.
The apple tree healed, leafed and flowered again.

And the Queen of Scrap? Recycled over the years,
soldered layers melding into each other,
hundreds of pounds of scrap showing the way.

10. Thin Ice

We didn't call it fear. Only ants
and spiders died. Not kids. And I was big.
I wandered to where concrete foundations deep

with winter looked like frozen ponds. Pipes
sticking up, studs blackened stumps,
the rink looked solid enough. Sliding across,

I fell feet first through thin ice, my burly
body a soggy, woolen, booted mass.
Brittle edges breaking, I fiercely twisted

and thrust my walrus body to the wall,
lurched for a pipe and hunched my way out.
I recall the going more than the coming.

11. Maybe the Rocks Did Soften in the Sun

Maybe the rocks did soften in the sun,
trees bow, dogs sprawl on the green tongue of the lawn.
I know I hid in the high leaves of the apple,

listening as notes flowed out the piano's mouth,
the sole stirring, and took me to a cave
where I heard the echo of myself bounce

from wall to wall, the reverberations plunging
into the mysterious heart where harmonized
with cicadas the self settled and sang.

Ghosts of childhood flit through the leafing trees.
If we look back, we change, but not to stone,
this poem the severed head that keeps on singing.

12. A Coded Calligraphy

The trick, to pick out patterns in the skies,
the scattered stars a coded calligraphy,
to draw eye lines around the Little Dipper,

and the Big — sitting on the deck, Dad's arm
around me. Indoor light deepened the dark
and made the sky more readable. Moonlight

sluiced the bay in burnished gold and ripples
wrote on sand. A warm breeze folded us
in August. I never named the heroes and beasts

that tramped the skies, and the script of comets
hypnotized, but the tale of insignificance,
us inside the others, became my own.

13. Fishing With Bamboo Pole

Fishing with bamboo pole. Single string.
One hook. A bobber. I bait the line, and hunch
over the bay singing to snappers angling the bow.

Here is the place to wander, where frontiers vanish,
where anchors drift, and a purple evening unscrolls.
Not one word swallows the hook of time.

Even the slapping of water is in the mind.
Slit eyes do not delimit space —
mind and imagination meet in watery earth.

A far off thrill of breeze creases the bay
and the hollow wood taps against an oarlock.
Hearing floats on silence. The mind casts off.

14. Catching Shiners

At first more than bait, they'd swim close in
at low tide, darting sharp silver angles,
the bright tingle fretting the shallows.

Elements into emotions. We wanted them.
We each held a pole, the net taut between,
one end fixed. I waded out ninety

degrees from you. The silver churning, the fast
wade forward, the closing, the scoop, and a school was ours.
In a bucket of water, beauty became bait.

A microcosm where Being corrodes. Where freedom
is pulling away as waves are not water.
As silver angles decorate amphora earth.

15. Australopithecus

Australopithecus — the leafy lair
a simian memory, safety in grasp and swing,
but now she forages into no-man's land.

Toes got me in and out of trees, crunched hard
against the branch for balance, angled fin-like
through the surf, hooked for cherrystones.

While you on point. Pirouettes came natural.
(You might have been an athlete somersaulting
across the backs of bulls. Or temple dancer.)

The footprint of summer 1939:
your toes turn on the radio: Nazis invade
Poland. The news from no-man's land begins.

16. Disparates

Like Hermes soldered in the stained glass pane —
athlete, envoy, guide — we are a mix of disparates.
I open the door to a dirge of straight-backed chairs.

Wreaths and a cross flower around the coffin,
and murmuring shades ebb and flow.
At once a small man moves to where I stand.

Your father's at the river that crowns the City.
Its waves of watery suns reflect the eyes
of hovering angels posted at the gates.

What? Symbols loom where death begins,
but if the stories extract pain from loss,
yes, myth, to balance dirt thrown on the box.

17. The "Bridge of Sighs"

First 'home,' then 'house' after I lifted the chiaroscuro,
the "Bridge of Sighs," from the darkened wall, a light
patch left, a sign of filial treachery.

And then the division — carpets, mirrors, tables,
sofa, silver — just, but dismemberment
nevertheless, full reduced to empty,

an internment in the spoils of death. Each thing
bravely wearing her touch, its own history,
up to the last surrounded by its neighbors.

Now things, estranged, set up in another home
look somewhat familiar, like objects on the horizon's
sliver of light as the sun goes quickly down.

18. Dreams of the Red Brick House

The red brick house returned four times. Walls
doorless. A presence circling in the softly
stippled dark. The window above eye level.

A warning? Leave well enough alone? Memory
rejects change. Stained glass, with Mercury
the solder, is now a mustard-colored pane.

The sculpted columns of the once grand
mantel frame a brown electric heater.
Spacious rooms recede into their corners.

To funereal black the oak lintels of 'home'
turn as old truth dawns: return is a ruse,
a betrayal of things, a quaint opacity of age.

19. When Is Spirit Born?

When is spirit born, flashing like a fish
brightly in the human stream? And formed?
Swimming the channel or walking barefoot on shells?

Perhaps berrypicking where the thirteen tribes
wandered soft-shod on the fish-shaped island,
tail fins a harbor for Montauks and Patchoags?

According to its bent, it might track clouds
or stalk the sandpiper's lacey print. A fish
under the dock belly up is a fact.

It makes peace with the flawed shape of mind
and body, that strange amalgam that is forged
and forges, until the three are one. At the last.

20. "Paumanok"

Strike a note of praise and don't be shy
about what Walt and I thought singular —
Long Island, "Paumanok," floating off

the southeast New York coast, summers adrift
on your great tail flukes — Patchogue, Montauk,
Mattituck. I trapped the scurrying sand crab,

pulled against the snapper on the line,
tracked blue claw in the creek, and bodysurfed
the clouds. One harbors Eden for a lifetime

and measures places by its sun and sky,
its stillness where the shy deer sips and cows
pass by silently searching the salt lick out.

21. Triptych

Great Neck, Long Island, 1937

Once upon a time, we didn't believe
that beauty and horror could live "foreverafter"
side by side. Even the fabled beast
tending roses awakened from his spell.

We don't. The spell renews each time we list
the toys that take us past the line that war
divides. The shells you floated in the bowl
opened into paper lilies. The wooden
apple that fit into my palm, poured
a teapot out and cups with handles.
Toys from the country of the girls
in kimonos painted on puzzle pieces, fragments
of beauty waiting to be arranged.

Peconic Bay, Long Island, 1942

Under the August sun the deep green water
lisped quietly along the empty beach.
Trembled at the top of the white posts
of the dock that rose up over the placid bay.
Standing in saltwater up to my knees, I bent
over to splash myself and felt a nudge
on my leg, and turning, saw, bobbing behind
me, a green glass buoy, a colossus eye,
held up all day for its convergence
of green sand, green sky, green bay.

The evening radio news was a sober cipher
of cold Atlantic waters, boats and spies,
of Japanese fishermen off the Island's coast.

Eye-witness Reports, Hiroshima, 1945

Inside the temple Buddha began to melt,
an eye, a cheek, a nose, bronze bones fused
at odd angles. The priest resembled Him.

The convulsed sky broke into thousands
of clouds and in the interstices, blue sprawled
like morning glories across the heated air.

Whirlpools of fire pinwheeled through the city.
People, prickled with shards of metal and glass,
wandered blindly. We pried eyes open.

Where we touched, skin peeled. Then the rain,
black and cold. I snapped a picture of a woman
whose hand covered an eye like a pomegranate.

From a hilltop he saw the city turn yellow, then split
into night and day. The underside of the cloud
was rainbow. Later he remembered it as beautiful.

22. Pop

Up at 4 AM to hitch the horses
to the flatbed. Day in day out —
a "steady provider" was the phrase.

Black night lightens in the east
and sketches the first grey lines
of barns and stores.

Stable smells waft
from hooves shuffling on straw,
from yoke, rope, leather harness,

the sweat of men pushing
and pulling drums of kerosene
up the ramp onto the flatbed.

A clicking call, and the duo
softly neighing sets off,
the workmen grunting

encouragement.
The flatbed bellyaches
under its load

as Grandpa steadies it on its route.
Along what avenues?
Flatbush? Fulton past the Old Ferry,

snaking southeast, southwest,
then southeast again? Past
Whitman's RR tunnel?

Who knows the route another takes?
All we were told is that come Friday
night, when Pop got home,

he'd wash, put on his Sunday best
and walk down the block to O'Malley's.
A few rounds with the boys

and shortly after be carried home,
"stiff as a board,"
top hat in another man's hand.

23. Nana's Contribution to the English Language

Grossmutter, my mother called her — her immigrant face
sharp as a chipped stone, not at all like gentle Nana.

Who are the children in the photo? Mother, uncles. Then
Grandpa. And her. Nana knew how to hold things together.

Sunday dinner: the white linen cloth, the kind that needs
sprinkling and a heavy iron, and then the story of the stained

glass chandelier — broken by children in the morning and glued
together before her sedate husband came home from work.

Not a word. It spilled a sunset of citrus over the table, its baskets
of fruit overflowing with grapes, oranges, apples, peaches, pears,

in soft arcs of color, the cornucopia of a harvest
of summer crops festooned by garlands of ribbons.

Beneath on the table the home-cooked bounty — sauerkraut,
red cabbage, fricadellen, spaetzle, pork chops, sauerbraten.

They sat beneath its muted glow. Not a word. Discretion,
the virtue that removed burrs and sharp edges from dinnertime.

Silence, the glue that mended whatever hairline cracks
or flaws threaded the texture and grain of each day.

Ritual, the patina: platters rotated clockwise to
murmured chants: Please, pass the... Thank you... Thank you.

24. Where Judgment Bobs and Weaves

The first real test of courage I ever took
was lying on a trestle while the train
chugged by two hundred feet above the valley
floor behind the terrace where I lived.
A ladder of one-inch rungs led to a view
three hundred and sixty degrees above trees,
buildings, and boulevard, a dreamer's world,
where clouds like shadow puppets glided by.
I walked out to the middle, fifty feet
of fearlessness on a platform four feet wide,
until I felt the tension in the boards
and heard a metallic click riding the rails.
I turned. Truth loomed, non-stop, dark and strange.
I turned my back on it and dropped face down,
arms up over my head, the space of an eye
between each lacquered board, the road below
a careless string of shacks and rusted Fords.
I girded up: the 3:45 rumbled by
some damn fool kid face down on a trestle bridge.

—⟋⟍—

But can "once" reoccur? I dared myself
again, this time to descend the sandy cliffs
that lined the valley straddled by the trestle.
I knelt and slid my left foot back and down,
my heel against a clump of twigs, my right
toe wormed into the dirt above a stone.
The trick — to step, then shift my weight, and wait,
then slide my foot. The sandy crust up close
dissolved in fragile spines and troughs.

A circus of summer clouds marched through the sky,
but here, forehead clamped against the cliff,
was frightened life. A sudden stream of dirt
rained on my head. I stuttered both feet left
and dug into a patch of dandelions.
Clutching the cliff — my nemesis, my salvation —
I inched my way back up as chunks of dirt
and stones like cannonballs bulldozed gullies
and breached the walls of my airy castle
where no flags flew, no youthful heroine walked
the battlements, no trumpet sounded victory.

.—⚜—.

The years that followed ricocheted between
a modest rashness and caution, but still unlearned,
that mettle needs to fuse with common sense.
A decade later the soldering took hold.
I took another kind of plunge, this time
a coastal bus ride down the Sorrentine
Peninsula. I should have said no
to an antique yellow bus with half-filled tires,
a dented body, and leather seats with stuffing
coming out. The young bus driver, dark eyes
roving over my lone form, in a deal
with Saint Anthony to exorcize
the demons from my twenty-year-old soul,
swigged a drink, then took the wheel and drove
hell bent along a road that snaked across
high cliffs. Lashed to the wheel he heard the sirens'
song rise from the crashing surf below,

but the clatter of the bus on hairpin curves
deafened me and speed rappelled me down
the cliff of fear into an ether no astronomy
could name, where judgment bobs and weaves
on the tip of a pin, into a land where people
are not the shortest distance between two points.

SISTER CHRONICLES

Prologue

We know the stories of individual women — the myths about Helen of Troy, the biographies of Madame Curie and Christine de Pisan — but until recently we had no sense of their place in history because there was no history of women, and women were rarely included in the history of men, which was the history of the world. A small band of women, students most of them, at what was then San Diego State College, set out in 1969 to change that. At first they didn't know that was what they were going to do. At first they gathered together to seek self-knowledge, as well as knowledge about the conditions of other women's lives. They surprised everybody, and not the least themselves, when their introspection resulted in a carefully drawn up vision of a Center for Women with interlocking units (ponderously called "components" at the time) that together would reflect the complexity of women's lives.

> As if an iconostasis carved in whorls
> of leaves and beasts were lowered on the world
> and on the wall at sword-length intervals,
> arms crossed, stood bishops, judges, generals,
> hooded, severe, the women in meek thrall,
> bit players, walk-ons, seconds in the call
> to power: this they rejected out of hand -
> and looked within, and to each other, to plan.
>
> It may be flocks of birds surfed the desert breeze,
> a great fish pressed the coast, its spout
> a metronome for chimes, or sea birds rose
> from the lighthouse cliff in arcs of perfect C's —
> all welcome signs. Fact: Fire flared out,
> a fist of rage from hurt turned inside out.

Where to begin this story, as simply as possible? Perhaps in the mind of one of the women who before had always noticed which girls in school were "in," which ones were "out." Someone who at last was able to reject given roles, who grew clearer and clearer about herself, and who was delighted to discover that the whole truth about the world had not yet been turned in.

1. Arma Feminamque Cano
(Arms and the Woman I Sing)

Fed up with being history's missing link,
the document drafted in invisible ink,

our story now dead-centers on the page.
How to start? What tone? Words? What phrase?

"Arms and the (wo) man I sing"? "Oh wild west woman"?
"Midway in this..."? "Of woman's first rebellion..."?

Will matriarchal fancies do (menses
tracks the moon) or fiddling with subtle essences?

"WE" are innately friendly, good, kind?
Or, over the poem, loop a wreath with a sign

that asks: "What is woman?" (Too loose in scope.)
Maybe: "Who am I?" (I know! No doubt!)

Too late! Impatience wilts the brain! Let others
grapple with abstractions and wait for answers

to When is SHE unnatural? If her bicep's
more muscled than? Hips — hippier hips?

Her voice harsher than? Hair shorter than?
Face plainer than? When a freak? Can

breasts be larger? Nose more bulbous?
When a witch — those eyes a syllabus

of perceptions, sharper, more refined,
with ideas more acute, powers defined?

A SHE should be — what? Oh! They should be
redressed! Boudicca, Botchkareva, Dido,

Ng Mui, the Danaids... I... thee.

Unlike the history of women, the dominant cultural legacy
was not fragmented and discontinuous. It was all-pervasive,
stitched into whole cloth by institutionalized Christianity and the
traditions of the patriarchs. Its view of Woman, when stripped
of the boundaries imposed by the cult of Mary, is symbolized by
the sculpture of Frau Welt in the portal of the great Cathedral
of Worms in Germany. The front of the burgher lady is full,
charming, to be adored, a secular double of Mary; the back, a
malignant bag of maggot-infested flesh and bones, the eternal
disgrace of Eve. It was this view of Woman that needed to be
dismantled.

2. Everywoman

It is a fact that
smiling and sweet,
Frau Welt, burgher lady,
well-groomed, petite,
stands in the round
at Worms,
in a stone gown
cut in soft folds
that fall
from breast
to toes.

In one body
at least three:
Mary —
seedless womb
worshipped by seed;
Beatrice —
aloof-eyed
civilizer and guide;
and Helen —
who enthralled
strong men to war.

The sculpted folds
of the dress quickly tell
of modest breasts,
of hips and thighs

that gently swell.
Against draped knees
a knight sits and sighs,
his sharp sword
unsheathed,
ready to rise
for Love and God's Word.

⁓

It is also a fact that
a fourth joins the act:
gorgon in stone,
back and rump
naked,
battered
to a stump,
gutted by maggots,
eaten by toads.
Worms stitch up the flesh,
flies breed on bone.

⁓

There Devil's Gateway!
There Frailty!
Death's Deaconess!
O Hideous Tapeworm!
Vessel of Death!
Misbegotten Man!
Succubus!
It is you
Eternal Bride!
turned traitor
to flesh.

One fact remains:
a vile smell
exhales from that stone
in the south portal
where saintly fathers
pass in and out.
O mundas! mundas!
East West
North South
the perfume of decay
drugs every century.
Corrodes the purest entry,
until it gags the mouth,
turns heart and mind
to stone, reduces complexity
to a dogma,
a people
forced into a formula
that does not vary
from day to day,
here with us still
hundreds of years away.

But Christianity was a mere charismatic cult at first. It needed a political engine to drive it over the Middle Eastern and Western worlds, suppressing goddess cults, and conquering cultures that honored a wider range of public roles for women. That engine was the Roman Empire. The story of legendary Dido, no matter how slim historically, chalks up failed female leadership to lost love, for, after all, what other cause could there be?

3. Dido Did It

It was rumored Dido died
for love. Some call her virgin queen.

The truth may be in between.
In exile from Tyre, widowed by a brother,

she captained a fleet, with priestesses
and priest headed west with her goddess.

In cagey deals with a gullible chief
swapped ox hide strips laid end to end
for land as far as any eye could see.
Had sealed in terra cotta urns

the ashes of boys fed to Tanit,
to Her of lion heart and head.

(Dido walked on paving stones
with priestesses between the Tophet

and high sea cliffs. Dido walked
decorously past houses six floors

high on Byrsa Hill.) In scorn
of local marriage offers (whether

to save her city or herself
from male lust), the immigrant

mounted a pyre, stabbed herself,
then burned into a fiery dust.

In worship, sex, and politics —
blood sacrifice. In misogyny, too:

Carthage, Cato said, is doomed,
and Rome salted the seeded ground,

and it grew bitter as Dido's shade
when grapevines whispered "unrequited

love," and it fell silent as Dido's
shade walking the wood of wounds.

It was within Patriarchy — this oppressive complicity of art, literature, myth, history, all institutions — that the First and then the Second Wave was born. A unique and all–important feature of the Second Wave was the explicit effort to eliminate the split between mind and body. Our bodies — humiliated as "evil," "lesser," "repugnant," and "enticing" — were indeed ourselves.

4. Our Bodies Ourselves

Even Hypatia felt the body irrelevant
in light of "higher things," and to prevent
a student's looking on her face and form
rather than into his own mind, and beyond,

presented him, according to Damascius,
her bloody menstrual rag to change his focus:
The "One" requires that mind cease its chatter
and in that silence moves the final matter.

But contemplation moves us not beyond,
but into the body's paths, where we respond
to its circuitries, its stance, its blood and breath.
It cleanses us like high tide the beach.

The core of the problem, we were told, lies not in a woman's heart
— how open, generous, humane — nor in her mind—according
to many, she had none to speak of — but in her vagina — how
guarded, secretive, and pure. To gain more control over the
physical self, women not only repudiated the division between
body and mind, but also the imagery associated with that division.
One of the major images of virginity is the image, not of Mary the
physical mother of Jesus, but of the Virgin Mary.

5. Glad Tidings

These are how I want my wings to be —
not heavy thick-feathered floor-brushing wings,
too heavy for a twitch of disgust
or a slump of impatience,
but smaller more flexible ones, ribbed delicately
by a fine musculature
that allows for subtlety,
covered in fluffier feathers, calf-length.

I too would stand with one hand holding a draped cape,
the other with palm extended
upwards towards Mary,
but I would tell her to stop this nonsense —
interspersed with hosannas
circling my halo —
telling her at first joyfully,
while the sky is framed in a strange
celestial architecture, telling her again
with a twitch or slump of the right wing
that there is no sin,
that she can give birth
and not be virgin.

How could the vision of a Women's Center, and the creation of its first component, the Women's Studies Program, have their roots in San Diego? The Second Wave of the Women's Movement hit the beaches of San Diego in 1969. Some date it from right after the People's Park March in Berkeley, California. Two of the founders met through a mutual friend and discovered much in common: that the paths set out for women were often mindless and confining, yet defined for them at birth. They decided to bring some women together to discuss their lives and to read what was happening in other parts of the country. They did that and discovered others could be moved to action in their own behalf. Silence and passivity would no longer be their only legacy.

6. Song of Silence

Always in cars, at malls, timidity
chokes her, gentility
makes her smile and ask forgiveness
for sins, sins without badness.

Even her shadow is unsubstantial:
a silhouette stenciled
on nursery walls, gray lines
traced by children, strict rhymes.

Metaphorically speaking, she lives alone,
her family of cut-outs cloned
for square rooms and windows, closed
doors with no knobs, sealed.
Outside a cypress on one wall
sobs a tear shape, and a pall
of crows, guttural crowd,
swirls over the air like a shroud.

Inside the things of daily life
rise up colossal, a knife
against one wall, a comb and brush
to hold the ceiling up.

In the window, a wink of light
flutters the curtain of the night.
All is silent, dark and cold;
the air, heavy and stale, old.

~

Memory becomes history
if it goes beyond one story.
Includes strangers. Is designed
to stir collective mind.

If so, she has no history.
Just journals, zigzags of memory —
her first kiss, graduation day,
getting a job in L.A.

No women gather on her pages,
no Zenobias or Hypatias
grace her shelves. No list
including 9:45 a.m. — PROTEST!

Life, a blood-red rose, blooms
wildly, its petals filling up rooms,
overflowing windows and door,
stifling her, more and more.

There was no turning back. The path to the center of things would have to be approached more boldly. And if no sanctuary could be found, they would have to build their own — no one would do it for them.

7. On the Path to Athena Proneia

At the center of Earth
there was no light
the only sound our feet

and from the hill above
a warm night breeze
wove through our words.

We strained to see through
the olive trees the ruins of
She-Who-Was-Here-First,

to stone on stone that
honed spirit before the memory
of man, that said there was

more than manly beauty.
We could not. Our faith lay in
our faith the stones were there.

If the moon had been more than an arc,
if the faithful had gathered pure
from the sacred flume to watch

the circle of flames that cracked
open the night, we would have touched
the site. But we were two women

alone
afraid to enter the dark
cut off from sanctuary.

Just as women from our real and legendary past were being resurrected, just as the first rays of a possible history of women glimmered in the distance, so many women, living among us, hurt in profound ways by nightmarish lives, tried to resurrect themselves.

8. The Snake of Hurt

the snake raises its head
the skin of the snake
begins to shed
twisting to get free
it stretches into fear
the pit is full of snakes
anguished lair
no doctor presides
no god dazzles the night
to purge the mazy mind
no priests chant
prayers for the soul
god is the snake is them
the mask of pain
its open mouth
its eye of terror
mounds of twisting
pains that hiss
Heal me! Heal me!

No matter where we came from, there was only one path to the sanctuary where healing could begin in the company of sisters — and that path was through anger and rage. Few escaped this route.

9. The Danaids

Defiant are the Danaids of
one-hundred breasts, holy sisters

forced to leave an ancient worship
who in righteous self-defense —

after the marriage feast, the drum
and flutes, the pungent myrrh, after

the purple robes that billowed bell-like
in the northern air, lorded

over by the hawk's ceaseless
wheeling across the cloudless sky,

after the wine and vows were swallowed
and those predatory wings dropped

darkness over the lit torches
that staked out the god's targets,

when dragged by their men
(already the fine hairs raised)

into the bridal chambers
and laid in the marriage bed

to receive the stamp of wife —
knifed and knifed and knifed again

the heated flesh until hot blood
ornamented sheets and walls
like roses scattered festively
across the twitching torch light,

who then upon the threshing floor
glutted with garbage from the feast

threw off their clothes and cleaned themselves
in consecrated wine, then danced and sang,

caroused to flutes and drums until
the sliver of the sun aroused

their hearts to prayers of victory
and praise. Their covenant reaffirmed,

they took sheaves of ritual wheat
from out of a cache and piled it

before their feet, and kneeling down
before the dying luster of

the hearth, before the dying purple
shadows, prayed to the mother of rain

to return again their power to them,
to force the hawk to head for shelter,

to wash away the stain of joy,
of guiltless consummated hate.

Their own world and the world around them, the past and the
present and the future, were talked about in Consciousness
Raising groups, until one day one of them suggested that perhaps
the proper study of womankind was Woman. The memories of
those days, even before the conflicts that caused so much anguish,
when sisterhood was new and powerful, are seen even now
through a many-colored prism of exhilaration and pain.

10. No Way!

Those were not the "good old days." No way! Too hard!
Look! Battle scars — stiff back, a fractured heart.

We came together on Forty-Seventh Street,
in bare-bones rooms, a student-style retreat

where R. A. lived, rental unit style — white chips
of paint, blond plastic furniture, rust spots on water taps —

disparates, desperate, a motley of women, CR'd to death,
to plan for change, lay claim at last to half the earth.

The summer sun blasted the dirt-patch yard (the only
green the weeds, a straggly tree, one loud but lonely

enthusiast, a barking dog, warning the bearded
god that thunder clouds scrolled west), bordered

by a picket fence, daydream of another era,
its boards nicked and cracked, in places held by wire.
We must study women, M. J. said. Yes, Ma'am!
Adam's rib? The better half? The little woman?

The woman in *a man works from dawn to sun,*
a woman's work ... ?

Yes, yes, that woman, that one.

Why not start a Women's Center at the local state college. A
Center that will provide services and identify resources for
women. But in San Diego, many women sneered? Here in San
Diego? A totally unknown place? A Hollywood movie set?
Not Chicago! Not New York! Not even Philadelphia! A place
referred to on the state arts map as Region V, Southern California:
Everything south, the desert, and all the rest...? Here? But the
founders said, San Diego is where we live and work.

11. Everything South, the Desert, and All the Rest

The Stereotypes

Here we learned what we were
up against, where to start,
who we could be in this city
of backcountry, bays, and border.

Here wasn't movie reels
of palm fronds and sand,
of boy-meets-girl, he sings,
she falls head-over-heels.

Or Westerns: Jimbo, grizzled,
boozed up and surly, brawls
& Ole Sal's gotta haul
'im home, drunk, brain frizzled.

Or superstars (the clichés just
don't quit!) in lotus poses,
levitating, noses
breathing cosmic dust.

Point Loma

Here was where herons catch the rise
in a whistle of wind that slaps the rocks
tumbled below in pounding surf
and seagulls circle their edgy cries.

Where herbs border the stony pass
past Loma's graves, where war dead lie
chirping their secrets secretly
to drifts of daisies and green grass.

San Diego Harbor and the Pacific Ocean

The harbor floats by our town
and flecks of light at night fall
from skyscrapers like shredded foil
on sails and water, shimmering down.

And crashed on hot summer days,
bathers drift off, swaddled in beach,
spines welded to the summer heat,
the horizon feathering into haze.

The City and Its Quirks

Quirks, yes, a mix of this
and that: where the "Fountain
for the People" in Horton Plaza
sprouts a finial acanthus

on top of a tripod to Dionysus,
and some of Kate's own twenty plus
palms still stand. Where a Wobbly
got tarred-and-feathered. Navy surplus.

The oomph behind this city's flare
lies also in geometry.
Buildings stacked in abstract array
of circles, triangles, and squares.

In streets all winding to a goal —
assemblages of art, and walks
pulsing music, and harbor paths
lit up by fireworks— each stroll

to delight. As if the Muse
declared a zone of song and dance
and beauty here in our city,
and invited us to join the dance.

12. Our Beautiful Back Country: Sloan Canyon Songs

The Arrival

Dawn, and the crouching sun breaks over the hill
to flash a signal to the chaparral

and to the uncoiling vertebrae of rock.
I glow as I hit the crest, then suddenly drop

from chest to feet
into a brushwood sea where manzanita

waves a warning at my gun, at the hostile
nimbus of the steel barrel.

Shooting at Cans

The sparrow hawk
marks off an arc
then props herself
against a shelf
of air. Hawk
eyes stalk me.
As I aim
at a can
I sense the fling
of spotted wings.

The Mine

At midday we reach a mine
dug by some old rough
who plodded months at a time
for gold. Milton stuffs
dry brush into a branch hollow,
lights it, and leads us on.
One by one we follow
into the catacomb:
a processional of eyes
and fingers touch the vein
that bleeds along the wall
and down into the groin
of earth, where, as legend
has it, the miner, his veins
turned gold, remained.
Earth lays the final claim.

Green Valley Falls: A Source of Legend

I emerge from scrub into an airy kitchen,
a stone peak grooved with rock bowls.

A crow drops through the air,
its sentinel caw sounds imagination.

Perhaps it is the woman who ground seed
where I stand now,

Green Valley stretched in vast directions.
I imagine manzanita a purple gown

and strands of gray hair braided
with the river curving down

through rocks to tumble in
disordered knots into the falls.

From a distant pine
she calls me, her cries

the last glimmer in the cooling air.
This is why I left camp

lured to the rocky edge
to watch her finish daily tasks,

then, balancing tool and basket
in the carrying places of her waist,

wrap herself in shadow
and descend the distant ridge.

The Region

Before hotels and condos paved
over vineyards, farms, and orchards,
before light-skinned gods tracked
the cache of Aztec gold northwards,

the tribe-of-eight-homes, the Dieguenos,
tracked the sun and watched its
gold fill up the harbor's groves
then light the caves with sunbursts.

All the gold there was was that,
and where acorns fell and sycamore
blossoms lured wild birds to traps
on hills reflected in the harbor.

Today music fills the niches
of the town, and people rethink themselves
in art and steel, and festivals
replace the shrinking place of nature,

but the river still rushes through its valley
with a murmur of stories, and lizards dive
through boulders scattered like debris
from comets shooting across the sky,

and cool desert winds still blow hot
from pell-mell treks down mountain slopes,
and white-throated swifts in flocks
whip through the air like snapped ropes.

This is *everything south, the desert,*
and all the rest — a city, core
of a golden region, a retort,
a story in sun and land and lore

But why did our dream demand more than just an Academic Program? After all, wouldn't that be the most obvious choice for an educational institution? The answer was simple. From the outset, in the Summer of 1969, it became clear to many of the women on the Ad Hoc Women's Studies Committee that women's needs are not isolated but rather interlock in many subtle as well as obvious ways. Had they not in the original CR rap groups in 1968 discussed the problems of women on welfare, in prison, on the job site, and in various other circumstances? In spite of pressure from certain groups to focus on just one issue, the structure the planning group conceived included the creation of a variety of components: Academic, Research & Publications, Recruitment, Tutorial, Cultural, Child Care, and a job-and-crisis-oriented Community Storefront. These were the ones listed on paper. Put into action, but not official, was an Underground Railroad for battered women, an Arts Festival that lit up the community for more than ten years, and rape crisis counseling before it had a name.

13. Why One-Dimensional Woman?

Expanded — in spite of SWP pressure
that we nibble one issue at a time

and then I asked her
whose? hers? yours? mine?

Did she prefer rape? abortion?
history? — what was her pleasure?

Where was she when the passion
took us to clamp a shell over

one ear and listen past the murmur
of waves breaking on the world

shore for the inconsolable whimper
of the woman on the kitchen table,

a crucifix of knitting needles
hanging over her, for the sullen

look of other women, riddles
of silence, eyes black and swollen?

What histories had she read?
The armies enter Country X,

down over the plains spread
like a rip tide — victory, success.

History: the march-across-the plain,
the allegiance sworn, treaties, trade —

not women raped, children slain,
not fields burnt, towns flayed.

Had she stood beneath the tree
and seen leaves drop, diseased,

she'd have seen the stain
spreading out into each vein.

Envoy

O pardon her who could not see
leafless forests for the tree.

The members of the Ad Hoc Committee for Women's Studies
explained their intent on a widely circulated petition. In February
of 1970, the SDSU Student Council adopted a resolution
supporting the Center for Women and its Academic Component.
Trial courses, already set up that spring in preexisting classes,
were thus given the stamp of approval. A temporary faculty
advisory committee would later add further legitimacy to the
autonomous program, as well as acting as liaison between the
Program and the College of Arts and Letters.

14. Notes on Actions and Auspicious Signs

- 40 women circulate 40 petitions
- 600 signatures
- presentations to Student Council
- Council supports Center concept

(The faithful know that oranges burst from blossoms on the tree.
The fragrance signals spring, as does the honeybee.)

- some confrontations, then more
- negotiations with V.P. for Academic Affairs
- result — 1.5 faculty positions
- sub-committee approval — full faculty approval

(Grey whales appeared along the coast, and oranges on trees:
the human season pleases most when it conforms to these.)

- more politicking — just in case
- words, words, words
- STAY THE COURSE!

(Grey whales complete their yearly swim to Baja's bays of love,
at least no salt spills on the shores, just traffic jams above.)

- springtime trial courses
- classes full
- at last!

(A further sign! Migrating jays flew due east from the bay.
Cacophony for two full days before they flew away.)

Finally, all that was left was the Great-Assembly-of–the–Suits-
and-Pipes and their vote of confirmation. When that took place,
Phase I was over, an effort so exhausting that the numbers on the
Ad Hoc Committee for Women's Studies had dwindled to about
ten women, nine students, and one part time faculty. The women
sat in a row on the auditorium stage, lined up like beer cans on a
fence.

15. Thus Spake What's-His-Name!

And thus he spake, in catchy phrase:
him rising in sartorial rage
us lined up in chairs on stage:

The hand that rocks the cradle rules the world.

(Were Mother's hands on Alexander's cradle
as potent as his battles?
Exchange the world for a cradle?)

No, we said, the hand that holds the rock...

Knowledge is power! Nam et
ipsa scientia potestas est.
Will and Idea are where it's at.

The proper study of Women is Woman!

Chewing laurel and sniffing fumes
on her tripod the oracle croons
yet another Delphic tune.

From the rocky gorge the route
of words drift through a mouth spout
twisting phrases inside out —

there are rocks in that cradle
rock the cradle
that cradle rocks
that hand handles a rock
rock on! rock on!

The women's proposal — even to themselves — looked at times like drifts of words scattered over an abyss of silence, of discontinuities and fears, of scattered mythologies that ended as subplots in the legends of heroes — an attempt to create a false coherence out of an historical incoherence. But they set it forth, and defended it, point by point. And at last the predominately male faculty voted thumbs up!

16. On Their Behalf

On their behalf, yes
(let me admit it) —
they voted thumbs up!
it does them credit.

An idea barely sketched
on R.A.'s front lawn
on 47th Street
took fire & form.

Inspired by seeable models —
Chicano, Black — but even
so, a verbal joust.
At last, the study of women!

Each discipline critiqued,
examined for relevance,
each interrogated
for its sense and nonsense.

Once owned by Others —
history, art, lit —
released by us to use
as we saw fit.

(As the Lethe in our minds
receded from its bank,
poppies lost their bloom
and the dull god's palace shrank.

Grand once in shadows,
it vanished as the light
of consciousness stirred
us from our sluggish night).

A poignant, some said,
enlightened vote: the state,
minions of the state,
were pressed, and it took place.

So a new idea
stamps an institution
(a negotiated settle-
ment) with its passion.

Oh, we rocked and rocked the cradle!

Down to a handful of women on the Ad Hoc Women's Studies Committee, who did all the leg work to implement the Center's first component, with the instructors hired, the Women's Studies Program was ready to start with classes full (in the Fall of 1970). At this critical moment, a squall of vocal ideologues appeared, who, after pitched pseudo-parliamentary battles, succeeded in ousting the Founding Mothers. They brought with them abstract ideologies to explain why they didn't like this or that, but most of all they didn't like the fact that they weren't in charge, even though they intoned that "no one should be in charge." Using leveling rhetoric, such as "open to all women," "elitism," "top heavy bureaucracy," "tainted money from foundations," and so on, they gained control of the recently established Women's Studies Board, and, after a fall semester of bitter assemblies, voted to separate the Women's Studies Program from the Center. The Center, however, instead of caving in, continued to provide programs for women in the community as well as on the campus. But who were these short-sighted spoilers? Many, especially the leaders, had political axes to grind that were not necessarily related to women's issues. Their methods? Prearranging votes, gaining access to students and instructors, intimidating classes via a peripatetic "guerrilla theater," and stacking voting assemblies. The Women's Studies Program, once under their control, lasted a few years, and then died, only to be reborn, after they cleared out when their schemes fell through.

17. Guerrilla Theater by Gorillas

None seemed more "forever,"
like trolls of the river
between whose ragged rocks
the vicious current traps
unwary boaters knocked
this way and that.

They were here to stay,
a dwarf majority
and their slanderous tracts —
name calling, creating facts
from lies (as if they'd read
how-to in a guide) — dead

cuts to the bone —
seem etched in stone.

Ideologues
of the monologue,
conference crashers
and trashers,
so they in classes
staged guerrilla masques
to parody & harangue
those who brought change;

loomed, dark shades and coats,
arms crossed, to bulldoze votes;
Coughed up charges, lists
of "ic's" and "ist's" —
"elitist," "bureaucratic,"
"undemocratic."

Their "mocracy" was born
from a tree gnawed down
to float a ship of state
on votes prefixed by hate
and talk behind the back —
the sharpened axe.

From those blows the tree
bled into the scree
and the spirit cut inside
cursed the enterprise:
Let vines entrap sails,
ivy hang from oars,
the crew, embalmed,
drift becalmed.

Abyssus abyssym invocat.
(They fell apart after that.)

Off campus, the Center, now called the Center for Women's Studies and Services (CWSS), established Sisterhood Chapters at state and local prisons and work camps, where the goal was to replace rivalries with sisterhood and raised consciousness. In 1971, the Center published one of the first all-women poetry anthologies, Rainbow Snake, including work by local poets as well as by such luminaries as Alfonsina Storni, Bella Akhmadulina, Diane Wakowski, Alta, and a supportive Anne Sexton. On campus, one of the first actions of the Center's Sisterhood Chapter was to mount an all-women arts festival in the SDSU library — five floors of art. The first festival in 1970 had a grand soft sculpture hanging down the main stairwell -- five floors of cascading red balloons and white sanitary pads. This sculpture initiated an on-going dialogue with the generous library staff over certain "problem" sculptures that inevitably appeared each year over the thirteen years that the Center put on the art show, an extravaganza participated in by hundreds of women artists from around Southern California.

18. Every So Many Days

Gifts of the Moon — the snake, the tree, red rain,
mata marama, black stone and sacred plain,
the omphalos, our authority over creation,
it means a helluva lot — menstruation.

(Helen, a girlhood friend, the fifth in a line
of four brothers, never received a sign.
A lucky few of us got onset gifts,
and congratulations, but still, bloated breasts.)

Why "the curse"? (Mary didn't have it?)
Can you believe 5 T. of blood make us invalid
when all it shows is Nature's acuity
in reminding us of our ferocity?

Incapacitated? Did Mussasa's daughter,
Tembandumba, who killed lover after lover
and ground male children into magic ointment
stop warfare during menses, impotent?

Chloris didn't break her powerful stride
on the plain of wild olives where Olympia lies
because of menses but went on to win,
hair free, breast bare, the first Heraean.

(Even I jogged — so it was Day Three —
on the plain outside Hera's sanctuary
between Alpheios and Kladeos,
not sprinting, it's true, but at my own pace.)

—⟋—

Cut to 1970: after eons of cramps,
there in the college library, a chance,
and space, for women artists to set up
whatever catharsis in art there is for us.

And it was grand! A soft sculpture filling
the stairwell four stories high: cascading
white sanitary pads and red balloons—
power of Menses, pull of the oval moon.
No more suffering for us! No more
spiritual slanders would we endure!

Even the most immune to sentiment
wept a silent tear at our disinterment.

(The library staff who summoned us looked glum
at the first of many such mediations,
the last the year the great pop penises
appeared in uncircumcised naturalness.)

The body can be good incarnate: that's all
there is. The woman In the poster lolls

(the artist her own delayed exposure)

head down, coiled around the branch and fruit,
the serpent skin discarded at the root,

(Woman is-s-s-s god is-s-s-s...)

her eyes dart through thick green leaves, her tongue
hisses the naked vowels of affirmation.

(i-u-i-u--us-s-s-s-i-u-i-u)

Finally the body breaks into its song:

I am the only god of right and wrong.

19. Meditation on the Maelstrom

If before a doctrine imposed
conformity, before the attacks would start —
and we tore ourselves apart,
if, before some of us Founding Mothers, bruised
and too tired to go on, withdrew,

leaving the coup to be fought by the few
left, had we known the viciousness
and disarray, that our own kind would curse us
as an old evil that leaves no shadow at noon —
would we do it again? Would we continue on?

The foundation was built: this was our consolation.
We found ourselves living through historic times,
and, yes, we'd do it again, albeit with caution.
We were not fair weather women: you tough
it out when the sky opens and seas get rough.

We lived to see the world as habitat —
our kind in technologies, in arms, a flight
of rage seasoning the race. To see a habit
reversed: to demand survival by natural right
in spite of the brutalities of abuse.

To see us rise on animal spirits born of use,
and we praise the circle of women, the counsel of friends,
and the high adventure of our own legend and truth.

20. Envoy

Compassion Goddess, let this be
a clean sweep of our history.

Pardon her whose revolution
boiled down to retribution.

Pardon her who shouted slogans
covering up a taste for pogroms.

Pardon her who dished out grief,
now a rose between her teeth.

Pardon her whose third degree
prepared her for psychology.

Let this be their *in memoriam*.
For them all: Rest *in pacem*.

MT. HELIX SONGS

1. Crow's Fault

It was the crow's fault.
It flew in at midnight,
its shadow the shadow
of cloud, tree and post.
But not of moon. The moon
was a cracked egg in the sky.

Throughout the night it dozed.
Then as the thin milk of dawn
coated the earth, it stirred, its caw
a repeated whisk,
a repeated swirl of moon
into sun. Bright. Brighter. Brightest.

It poured sun on the griddle
of streets. Day puffed up,
a soufflé, a baked blend
with bits of house, walk, and hedge
folded into the rising mix
until it set, brown at the edges.

2. After the Squall

After the squall,
in spite of carefully caulked
double windows,
in spite of inspection
by magnifying glass,
one tiny tear of water outfoxed
the sharpest eye,
dripped down inside the south
wall like a small
anger breaking through,
one miniature wrath at a time.

Absolute as sky.

3. It Will Turn Out To Be Another Spring

No flowers, no berries on the walls of air
that float above the garden. Spring skulks
beneath cloud cover, not even splitting bulbs.
I hook the feeder on a shepherd's crook
to coax birds to the garden strip where
risers water decomposing mulch.

My part in the round is no mystery.
As a girl, I didn't climb a wild trail to a
cave where fantasies and thoughts
flickered on the wall, then crouched,
it seems now, days and nights in a tree,
mulling over what happens to earth happens to me.

The light changes: the pachanga* should start soon.
Birds will convene and the looked-for rite
of lily, rose, dianthus begin. May they bloom
full bore! Orange trees will frizz white
and grapevines slaver in the sun. Bees buzz.
Something will happen to me — it always does.

"Pachanga" means "a bash" in Spanish.

4. The Wrentit

Shuffling between whiskers
of chaparral -
sage, coyote brush,
a scurry, a peck and rush,
a jerky shuff -
le, a long tailed dust-
ing of dirt, a dit-dit-dit-t-t-
t-t that crests
in a leafy flutter
like mind
behind face -
a cover.

5. The Three Foxes

I discovered how they got in,
an alley between fences, sliver
enough for one, single file.

Backyard marauders who ditched
mom at the neighbor's
down the street on Frontage Road.

I watched night games
through the window — racing the cat
or silent steps

with necks arched, eyes aglitter,
flickering fireflies caught
for a spell in summer hands.

A morning intruder, I startled —
sleeping under the deck,
curled into each other like children.

A standoff then, they
at one end of the path, me
at the other, sizing each other up.

The trio, black stripe, bushy
tail and low growls, monitored me.
They had the run of the yard.

The Possum Lady said,
"Enjoy them.
Don't feed, just watch. When
they've eaten what stirs,
they leave."
They'll leave and you'll be sorry

not to catch the glint,
to see them tighten into balls
and roll down the lawn.

Remnants of nature are left.
Words. What they are
vanishing into tapering corridors.

6. The Santa Ana

Santa Ana winds blast down the mountain passes
from the cold desert and burn us in fury.
Caws of crows shred the trees, the sound whirligigs
into the sky, mountains tooth the sun.

We're stretched over the city, its parched skin.
We stay indoors, stop exercise, drink lots of water.
As if this could stop weather. As if flowers wouldn't fry
and days sprawl in endless loll,

and minutes pop like stewed berries.

7. The Wild Parrots

The wild parrots flash like green and red
boomerangs over our cape chestnut,
its pink flowers crushed against the sky.

The story goes that they were tame
once, in cages, listening day after day
to "Avast, m'hearties" and "Yr arse!"

They didn't come through, didn't want
to repeat stale crackers of language
and were petulantly let go to travel

on sibilants of wind, over hieroglyphs
of tree tops, rolling around in small
swirls of weather, a chattering tribe

camped on the edge of town. They whiz
here and there on hot winds
from the Point or eastward during squalls,

settling a while in the chestnut
and gingko just sprouting nubby twigs.
They squawk at silver eucalyptus leaves.

Never for an instant is there silence,
as if all earthly engines were tuning up,
as if there were never too much time

in which to talk about our lies,
flashing back and forth scrawling circles
over the house, over the city, over the coast.

8. The Back Yard

Isn't this
the way of things —

Our yard, its back
turned on urban gaud,
burnished to park.

Its blood rose,
a red Don Juan,
climbing the trellis of sun

like the mind
entwines
innocence.

Above the white gazebo
sprawled with a purple vine
akimbo

hovers the angel,
really an angle
on imperfection

watching innocence,
its unleafed resonance,
leaf into cycles.

    Mallards, tan
    and green, drop in
    and mate.

A midnight raccoon,
bandito cadger,
raids the garbage.

Barn Owl, a haunt
in pink puffs of flowers,
hunts.

Flaming up, firethorn
cuts the air,
but we're still here —

life chases its tail.

9. Just To Be Sure

With friends to help, I dug some holes,
positioned the plants, mulched,

tamped the damp dirt into place
and watered at the root.

Alone I sang a song to earth,
then glanced up at the sky

to greet whatever ear that hears,
whatever eye —

and for a secret, silent hex
(to nip it in the bud)

red wine sprinkled from a glass,
a dance, a bow, four signs:

arms stretched out, a circle, a cross,
just to be sure, an "X."

10. Tomatoes and Tomato Cages

Not Time - this poem is not about it -
and it's not about Death or Loss.

(My face is flushed from the sun
and my ears buzz with stillness.)

It's about tomatoes and tomato cages,
metal mesh in three six-foot bins

with spikes to grip the earth,
so not to blow over in the wind.

(My arms, lifting mesh to bend
and secure, harden.)

It's about manure forked into dirt.
A zesty mulch tools a garden.

It's about cisterns, sealed clay pots
dug into strategic spots.

(I conjure roots
sucking through tendril straws.)

It's about the neighbor next door
broadcasting maxims:

Plant too early, danger of frost.
Too late, by fall, spindly stems.

(Me on all fours
using hands as trowels.)
Plant just right, you taste sun,
she said, in the red fruit core.

It's about refilling the vessel
with silence and breath.

11. Proprieties

They pulled out rotted wood,
removed glass doors and windows
from the porch wall of the family room,
and left us living inside out.

All night the rain railed in gusts.
Wind pounded the spindly gingko,
its small green leaves shivering
in clusters on spur shoots,

and this morning jays scolded the blue
tarp nailed over the gaping hole,
as if a piece of sky had been ripped off,
and hung ninety degrees to dry.

We ate cereal in wool pants and coats,
grateful for the noisy company
that gave us an earful
about proprieties.

12. This Might Have Been Eden

Looking out over San Diego's Mission Trails Park,
once home to the Kumeyaay

This might have been Eden —

although Eden was groomed
with gourds and fruit trees, bursts
of yellow and orange and red,
a celestial festoon of blue,
and angels, their flaming swords
beveling the edge —

but a different kind —

in front of me the gorge
cuts Cowles and Kuai Pai into
twin humps and its river shambles
west from Eagle Peak to the bay,
sluicing pin oaks, clumps of reeds
and chaparral, a coastal ramble —

yet still pristine.

A mile away, no Eden —
streets, stores, school, and church
breathe us out, a fragile elsewhere wind,
in incubations of such dense artifice,
innocence is lost even to the eagle eye
and fruition blooms in gardens of the mind.

Or maybe this was better than Eden —

here nuts and fruit were eaten
and no one was damned,
only peaceful bands from gorge
to coast to mountains, and back again,
following food and seasons,
god, and lesser gods, but no scourge

of generations, just the deepened
grinding stones, and ceremonies
for crises, but when drought choked
the river's mouth and desert winds
blew pell-mell hot down the slopes
and few sycamore blossoms dropped

to line wild birds traps, all bore
the cataclysms of every place,
of every paradise where streams
dry up, fruit rots, summer birds vanish
into the winter sky, and the falling
light of noon fades into fires and dreams.

13. Living Over Leach Lines

Rainwater pours down the jagged mountain side, cascades
into gullies, rinses gardens and finally seeps
underground to mingle at lower grades
with ribbons of leach lines and leaks.
At the foot of the mountain, we've laid a basketweave side-
walk of brick. Our gardens, our house and gazebo
float over secret rivulets, a tide
with no ebb, just flow.

—

Our consolation is fantasy. Spinning tales rich
in history makes us lake dwellers, our hut
on stilts like cranes spearing fish,
a notched trunk to climb up.
Our dried lake bed is a lure to archaeologists
to sift through our remains, not stone pots,
silver earrings, one or two tusks,
but cell phones and lap tops.

—

A palazzo? Arcades of stone baroque front our quarters.
A balcony views bronze horses, quatrefoil windows.
Bridges skylark aromatic waters,
lapping the nose.
Dawn froths its latté over marble promenades and piazzas.
A gondolier, minimally sober, sings us to the dock.
A stray dog howls as the (allegro) pizzicato
comes to a paid stop.

Going Dutch, I'll steer my boat with its roof of grass
close to Reibach's Café, and drifting on light,
watch leaves swirling in currents pass
out of summer's sight.
In winter, if there's ice, I'll skate like a snow-clad ghost.
In spring, watch mimes do Rembrandt, stock still,
until night shades them into posts,
a voiceless nil.

.——✒——.

A preference - to watch my skin glow under northern lights
in St. Petersburg, pulled out of a marsh by Peter,
its palaces lathered in white nights,
granite lining the river.
Let's meet there next August, Dorogoy!* For the price of a ticket —
you bring bilingual Akhmatova, me, Brodsky —
a rendezvous on Nevsky Prospect
at Dom Knighi!

.——✒——.

Take comfort. No matter where, earth waters rush
beneath us. Like scattered islands, we float on lore,
with beast, rock, insect, bush,
around the molten core.
Take comfort. Myth breaks like fact from circling water
in magenta mantle, golden shield, cap —
so it confirms we raft the future,
the stars our only map.

I'm writing these lines sitting in my van. It's fall,
late afternoon, with faith in life and latté,
the sun weaker than noontime's ball,
listening to Respighi .
Three shots in the coffee, my second cup, working well.
Take comfort, friends, it doesn't get much better.
I rise with the music's swell.
I walk on water.

*"Dorogoy" means "Dear" in Russian; "Dom Knighi" is the name of a
Russian bookstore on Nevsky Prospect in St. Petersburg.

SAILING AWAY

1. Sailing Away

Moving out of the harbor,
wake streams like banners
from the stern. On deck I turn,

not towards the hot tub for two,
kisses and toasts, whoops
as the band strikes up,

but at the city as it etches
itself, an impromptu sketch
on the deck's protective glass.

A minute ago, Home red-tiled
County seat, three-masted schooners,
green lights on towers,

but now another city clones
itself on glass, the outline familiar
but ephemeral, off by a fraction

of an inch. Who lives in this city,
peaceful certainly, its burdens
lightened by transparency,

its ships airborne ghosts?
No trace of overbuilt hillside
careening to the coast.

Instead splashes of light.
Too soon to count its lacks,
its malfeasances and blight,

and too late to wait and see —
both cities razed in an instant.
I am at sea.

2. L. Had a Tube Placed Through Her Nose and Down Her Throat to the Esophagus In Order to Determine the Extent of Acid Reflux

Needless to say this technique
needs a tweak.

Meanwhile consider yourself a medical R2D2,
a unit-with-tube,

but you can still pick strawberries
and till the soil around the lettuce leaves

and rise above the ashes and offices
of each day's chores.

I hope you are not too uncomfortable —
about this or anything, L.

Think of our life as a grand vista
like the approach along the Sacred Way

to the tomb, the sun in a bright blue
sky like a Ming dragon hugging the avenue

of green lawns and parapets,
lined with statues of animals and bureaucrats,

vendors hawking postcards, orangeade,
buddhas with bulbs in their bellies, no shade

in the forest of tourists, me with a digital
crouching to get an upward angle,

not feeling Earth crawl off until
the carapace, moving like a giant turtle,

sooner or later conveys us all, chimeras,
into death's expanding and extravagant panoramas.

3. Listening to Mariachi Music at the Mission

Ai! Ya! The singer sobs into the summer air,
his voice a heartbreak
of slanting sounds

that rake the cobble stones
in the arcades, stir the bells
suspended like tears from the arches.

In the Mission square, red penstemon
and white matilja poppies
bow over the pond.

Ballads flower.

Violins weep to the four winds —
I am not nobody,

I am in love with you.
The guitarron strums,

No mother no father,
alone alone through the night.

Virgin of Guadalupe, protect us —
her gold banner flutters
under the cloudless dome.

Band after band, singer after singer
in the competition's rapt intensity
radiates over families on the lawn,

the melodies dying and rising like days,
the round of sorrow and joy turning
like the sombrero in the tenor's hands.

We sip our cokes keeping time even
to sorrow's notes. The baby next to us
chirps as his father kisses his neck.

The mother warns her two-year-old
not to follow the yellow butterfly down the path —
Come back querido dearest.

4. It's Very Clear

Why there and not here? From the Visitor Center deck the guide points out the ribbon of oak beyond the chaparral. The children wait, expectant, except for the eight-year-old whose thin voice unrolls like a breeze across the deck. *There's water over there. The trees follow the river.* And why two peaks on each side of the river? asks the guide. *The river cut through millions of years ago.* Rounding the elbow of the path down to the flat grinding rocks, I come across the group again, this time standing beneath a pin oak. A small voice drops like acorns from the tree. *There. Wood rat lairs — the funny humps that look like honeycombs.* The older kids gather and stare. He points with his stick and flips a stink beetle off the path. *Don't let him back into you or he'll skunk you.* Some people know everything, and, if they don't, they learn from wings of the red-tailed hawk soaring invisible currents — and use a stick to clear a path.

5. What Is Left Unsaid Is Said

"I sit alone on a rock by the stream;
the woods are deserted, full of autumn
feeling... " (From "The Four Seasons" by Chang Yu)

When Chang Yu says the woods are "full of
autumn feeling," he doesn't describe.
We know leaves like dead skin scale off,
the wind grinds to a cold edge,
leaf boats careen down mountain streams,
and the ground stiffens like a corpse.

What words leave invisible is visible.

Nor does he state feelings —
a filament of loss, old bones
skewered by pain, a throttling
of warmth, cheer turned to chips
of stone, the heart like bark peeling
from melaleucas.

What he leaves unsaid is said.

6. Every Part of the Birch Is Medicinal

We are
tree-crossed lovers. At the start
knotted by the Lady of the Woods,
enamored of white bark,

of the graceful
fall of branches, light green hoods
of leaves, and tubular catkin
sacks of fertility.

✍

I read
how prisoners in a land of birches have written
love poems from memory
on bark, their sole horizon.

And other folk
prayed to the genii in the tree
to send wisdom, but not to send
the Evil Eye or Devil.

✍

As a child
I stood in a circle of birches while a friend
carved me a cradle
of bark, with crisp curves and a fitted end.

And you
in another country grew up near woods, saddled

Krasny and rode among birches, the light
flickering a path through seeded silence.

∽

A tale is told
that one dark and moonless night
a man, asleep under a birch, warned by a Presence
of a storm at daylight,

bowed low
to the Spirit. Impressed with such deference,
It revealed a saying that would whisk
him home, if homesick in a foreign land.

∽

You never returned.
Cut off, homesick,
your heart was not a treeless island.
You planted birches in the niche
in front of
the window where a strand
of sunlight cheers the floor and wall.
Every part of the birch is medicinal.

7. Alone In the Desert

He unrolls from his bed,
a newspaper unfolded,
and checks himself into the day.

The news is this: the pain
at his left ear drains
down a stiffened neck

into a shoulder bone.
Slowly he orbits
the <u>Obit:</u> Not in one.

But now he's in <u>Op. Ed.</u>,
and what he says
goes: pain spreads

like a desert stretched
by unreachable gulfs,
a vastness over parched

relentless, wavy lines.
Head bowed, he declines
to kneel and pray.

On the back page, <u>Quik Bite</u>
scans no food light
enough to swallow.

What news there is, is grim.
So that's it.
The day has just begun.

8. The Empty Bottle
(With a smile for Ivan Turgenev)

A bank of gray clouds clogged the edge of the sky, but behind them streamed a vibrant blue of unique purity and force, and in the distance eddies of white wisps, broken off from the bank, hovered free, circling like birds. The sun stared through a clouded eye, and wind gusted and skimmed the trees. Ahead of me on the stony incline, hikers bent into their baseball caps. Hoping to catch up before they rounded the bend to the grinding stones sloped by the river, I walked faster, but my way was blocked by a form appearing suddenly like a caret in a written line.

A figure, my height, in broad brimmed hat, tan jumpsuit and scuffed boots, the tops unlaced, appeared ahead of me. Staff in hand she strode with straight back zigzagging along the rutted path. I stopped to swig a drink from my water bottle. The stranger stopped too, and tipped up what seemed an empty bottle. *Hiker,* I called out, *Stop and share a drink with me.* I repeated my invitation. She stopped and turned and grinned. *You again,* she snorted. *Have we met?* I asked. *Yes,* she replied, *we met as you rested on the white stone column base near the temple of Athena, dreaming of gods slipping from nature into human form.*

And I watched as you gawked, entranced by the great gold Buddha in Beijing, and saw you snap a picture, forbidden, and waited for Security to confront you. Your guide got you out of that scrape. She consulted her cuff, as if a list were written on it. *Glendalough on the greeny isle — I strolled with you across the bridge, paved with chicken wire to keep wet shoes from slipping, to the round tower, a refuge crusted with crosses, and at the Holy Well, where, long ago secret baptisms blessed the cruel air, I helped you help others fill their bottles with holy water.* By this time, she was standing straight on, hands on hips, as if scolding a small child. I didn't move. *I even retreated with you to the Abbey in the northern mountains of California where pine needles edge the stillness, and the gong of being wings into the forest and disappears.*

And in your own city sweated in the lodge where the flute anguished over the rising and falling of spirit, and heat from the steaming stones cleansed our lesser selves.

You have done all you can do. Not everyone is called. Not everyone wants to be called. Have done now. I have been drinking the water you offered me for years out of many bottles. Taunting me she held up her empty bottle and, in slow motion, waved it back and forth before my face. *It's empty! See?*

And with that she turned and gracefully moving into runner's stance ran off around the curve, and, when I arrived at the grinding rocks next to the swirling river choked near the bank with reeds, was nowhere to be seen.

9. The Village

My afterlife? Problematic,
unless dirt and worms and rain,
maybe some ash, are useful concepts.

Yours, however, seems quite upbeat:
bridges, towers, crystal domes,
blue skies, luminous beings hovering.

I say we split the difference and make
the here and now our future: streets,
if not of gold, lined with trees.

Walks and stores dappled in light.
A laugh, a cry — indifference rousted,
and justice, an opened window,

and our faces edged in brightness,
not wishful thinking (my point),
or hopelessness (yours).

NOTES AND SOURCES
ON THE SISTER CHRONICLES

[1] ARMA FEMINAMQUE CANO

Virgil's Aeneid begins with "Arms and the man I sing..." Other famous opening lines are parodied in this stanza.

Boudicca (d. A.D. 60), queen of an East Anglian tribe, led a revolt against the Roman occupiers of England.

Maria Botchkareva, leader of the "Battalion of Death," an all-woman unit, was one of the most famous Russian soldiers of World War I.

Dido, a princess who fled from Tyre in Phoenicia, is the legendary founder of Carthage in Libya who, according to Virgil, upon offering hospitality and love to Aeneas, committed suicide upon his departure.

Ng Mui, a Buddhist nun, along with Yim Wing Chun, are the legendary cofounders of the Chinese martial art Wing Chun. Ng Mui was said to be one of the survivors of the destruction of the Shaolin Temple by the Qing Dynasty (Seventeenth Century).

I have based my understanding of the Danaids on Jane Ellen Harrison's brilliant and innovative book Prolegomena, which draws on the appearance of the Danaids in Aeschylus's Suppliants, as well as on archaeological material. This understanding is grounded in a very early pre-Olympian layer of Greek religious thought in which the Danaids are portrayed as priestesses forced into an unjust marriage. The myths illustrate a movement from a matriarchal freedom into a patriarchal structure. I used the Merlin Press, London,1962, edition, based upon the 1903 and 1907 editions (pp. 613-623).

[2] EVERYWOMAN

The phrases in quotation marks are found in various writings of Church Fathers and others.

[3] DIDO DID IT

More on Dido: The main sources for the traditional patriarchal view of Dido material are Virgil (Aeneid, Book 1, 2, & 4) and Ovid (Heroides, 7: 1-8, and Metamorphoses,14: 75-81).

[4] OUR BODIES OURSELVES

Our Bodies Ourselves is a landmark feminist book written by the Boston Women's Health Book Collective, Inc., (Simon & Schuster, 1971). Many editions, and international distribution, have followed.

Hypatia, a Fourth Century A.D. pagan mathematician, mystic, and teacher, was dismembered by a Christian mob (c. 415 A.D.). Her father Theon was a mathematician and teacher at the Musaeum in Alexandria. A close friend to the Consul Orestes, both of whom saw eye to eye on the separation of Church activities from the state, Hypatia may have been seen as a pagan thorn in the side of the Church, a thorn that reduced the possibility of an accommodation between Church and State. I have read about her in the following books, among others: Socrates Scholasticus' Ecclesiastical History; Synesius of Cyrene's very readable Epistolae (Letters); a terse account in D.E. Smith's History of Mathematics, Vol.1 (Dover Edition, 1958, based on earlier manuscripts); and Maria Dzielska's Hypatia of Alexandria (Oxford Press, 1996), which cuts through the romanticism surrounding an eternally youthful and beautiful Hypatia, and makes a clear case for her being around sixty years old when she was murdered by a mob. Her dates are roughly 355 - 415 A.D. Hyptia received letters in Alexandria addressed simply to "The Muse." (This mini-portrait covers the sequence of poems elsewhere in this book called "Meditations on Hypatia of Alexandria.")

The separation of mind and body was part of the pagan neo-Platonic tradition, as well as the Christian tradition.

Damascius (480-550 A.D.), a Greek neo-Platonist, was the last of the scholars at Plato's Academy in Athens before it was shut down by Emperor Justinian. The fascinating detail mentioned here is from his Life of Isidore.

[5] SONG OF SILENCE

Zenobia was a Syrian queen who conquered Egypt (269 A.D.), ruling until 274. Defeated by Rome, she was taken there in chains, but because of her intellectual stature was granted freedom, a villa, and status as a Roman. She claimed descent from Dido.

[6] ON THE PATH TO ATHENA PRONEIA

The path to Athene Proneia, the sacred site of the Olympian goddess, was, in later Olympian times, the protective gateway to the temple of Apollo at Delphi in Greece. "Proneia" refers to this position. The omphalos stone found in the Temple to Apollo was, in Olympian times, thought to be the center of the earth (that is, the belly button of the world), but, in the time before the Olympians, where the ruins of Delphi are now scattered, that site was sacred to the cult of the Earth Goddess and associated oracles. This cult was associated with the healing water bubbling from the spring nearby called the Kastalian Spring. The poem specifically refers to the pre-Athena & pre-Apollo site, to the general area, as the "center of Earth." The layering of religion, and the consequent sifting of local goddesses through male and female Olympian deities, is at work here.

[7] THE SNAKE OF HURT

The snake in pre-Olympian times (long before 6th century B.C.), a symbol of death and regeneration, and, therefore, of healing, was associated with the Mother Goddess. In later times, Apollo took over many of her functions and, in fact, became associated with the healer Asclepios. Asclepios, in turn, was a personage later converted into a god, who has been accorded the honor of establishing a healing center at Epidaurus in Greece, around the 6th century B.C. The surviving basement of a round temple at the site is thought to have been for the housing of sacred snakes. (The caduceus, a staff with serpents twined around it, is used today to symbolize the medical profession.) Professor of Archaeology S.D. Lakovidis, in his wonderful guidebook Mycenae-Epidaurus (Ekdotike Athenon S.A., Athens 1981) describes some of the procedures of the healing center. In addition to therapeutic herbs and ritual cleansings, the sick would spend the night in the "hospital" and await the god's appearance in a dream which would indicate the prescribed treatment. Contact with the god would often shock those with nervous disorders into a calmer path. Physical exercise, baths, music, and a theater, a theater still in use today, were introduced at later dates. This most famous of ancient theaters, by the way, with more than fifty curving rows (seating capacity – 12,000) is so constructed that a whisper on the orchestra floor can be heard in the top row. The healing center expanded in size and reputation until 426 A.D. when it was closed by the Christian emperor Theodosius II (pp.127,130 - 135).

The modern day reference to a situation or a place as a "snake pit," that is, as crazed and non-therapeutic, is contrary to the connotation of healing, and is therefore yet another degeneration of an ancient link, actual and metaphorical, between nature and women, and men.

Why snakes? Snakes, their sloughing off old skin and acquiring new, are associated with death and regeneration. Their "underground" habitat gives them an imaginative mediation between the dead and the living, and between their physical being (on and in the earth) and plant life. All of these associations re-enforce their usefulness in prophesy. In addition, Merlin Stone in <u>When God Was a Woman</u> (Harcourt, Brace, Jovonovich, 1976) recounts instances of hallucinogenic and restorative effects from the venom of certain snakes (p. 213). Needless to say the negative connotation of the snake in the Garden of Eden tells us that a patriarchal ethos won out over those ancient Middle Eastern religions in which women prominently figured.

[8] THE DANAIDS

Please see Section [1] above.

[9] NO WAY!

"CR" refers to *consciousness raising* groups, a common vehicle in the Seventies used by women (usually no more than ten in a group) to discuss personal problems and topics specific to women, and to relate those problems and topics to the expectations and limitations imposed on women by the broader patriarchal society.

"CR'd to death" refers to our getting tired of talk, and moving on to action.

[10] EVERYTHING SOUTH, THE DESERT, AND ALL THE REST

This phrase, which ignored the existence of San Diego, appeared on an arts map published in 1977 by the California Arts Council. Some of us took umbrage.

Point Loma in San Diego is the site of a military cemetery.

Horton Plaza, given to San Diego by Alonzo Horton in 1870, is anchored by a beautiful fountain designed by Irving Gill based upon a Greek choragic monument by Lysicrates. Whether at the very top of the San Diego fountain there is a finial acanthus on top of a miniature tripod to Dionysus is open to debate.

Kate Sessions (1857-1940) was our very own horticulturalist and botanist who designed and planted Balboa Park in downtown San Diego, one of the most beautiful parks in the country.

The Industrial Workers of the World (the IWW), referred to as Wobblies, was a radical anti-capitalist union whose members were denied free speech in San Diego and run out of town. The incident involved arrests, police brutality, tarring and feathering, vigilante violence, Emma Goldman, and Ben Reitman, her partner, who was tortured and run out of town (Red Emma Speaks, Emma Goldman, Vintage Books, 1972). In 1912, free speech did not win the day in San Diego.

Navy surplus. San Diego used to be a predominately Navy town. Thus Navy surplus.

The "Sloan Canyon Songs" were first published in Year of the Fires, Joyce Nower (CWSS,1983).

"Green Valley Falls" originally appeared in Qin Warriors and Other Poems, Joyce Nower (Avranches Press, 2003).

Dieguenos Indians live in and around San Diego County in Southern California.

[11] WHY ONE-DIMENSIONAL WOMAN?

WSP refers to the Socialist Workers' Party, one of several groups in the early days of the Women's Movement that had their own agendas. Other such groups were the RSU or Radical Student Union and, later, after the formation of the program, NUC or New University Conference. The SWP representative at the very early meetings always talked about our executing just one action. We didn't follow that advice.

[12] NOTES ON ACTIONS AND AUSPICIOUS SIGNS

This strophe describes a part of the process that was used to establish the Women's Studies Program.

Gray whales provide a yearly spectacular in the months after Christmas off the shores of San Diego as they majestically make their way down the coast from the cold northern waters to give birth in the warm lagoons of Baja California.

[13] THUS SPAKE WHAT'S-HIS-NAME!

Yes, this actually happened!

[14] ON THEIR BEHALF

Lethe is one of the rivers in the Underworld or Hades (the world of the dead). One drink and you forget the past.

Hades is both a name for the Greek Underworld, and the name of the god who rules that place. The Romans called him Pluto. Hades was also referred to as the "dull god" because daylight did not penetrate his kingdom.

[15] GUERRILLA THEATER BY GORILLAS

Abyssus abyssym invocat. "Hell calls to hell," meaning "One misstep leads to another."

[16] EVERY SO MANY DAYS

The rainbow snake, as feminist mythologist and poet Barbara Mor wrote in the Introduction to the poetry book of the same name, "is one form of the cosmic serpent who appears universally in primitive and pagan mythology as the consort of the Great Goddess. Ancient rock engravings on Woman Island in northwest Australia depict female figures with triadic magic rays proceeding from their vulvas. Above them arcs the rainbow snake. This sacred relationship of woman and serpent found in all the major myths of the world originates in a time before patriarchy when women guided the cultural lives of their people, and when deity was conceived in female form" (Rainbow Snake, CWSS, printed by Grandma's Camera,1971).

The moon is traditionally connected to women and women's menstrual cycles.

Trees are significant in the world's mythologies: for example, in Greece, Egypt, and elsewhere in the Middle East -- fig, apple, and black mulberry. Robert Graves in The White Goddess tells us that trees played a fundamental role in the Druidical religion, stretching their mythy branches to all parts of the world (Farrar, Straus & Cudahy, Inc.,1948).

Red rain, exhaustively and scientifically explained at online Wikipedia, stands for what you think it does. It is a perfect example of how a metaphor is born.

Mata marama or menstruation, or "moon sickness," is a term used by the Maori of New Zealand.

The black stone is an ancient pre-Islamic image of the Goddess.

The omphalos stone at Delphi, the most famous "center of the earth," is associated with the female oracle there, and pre-dates the Olympian conquest of the female deities.

Tembandumba, the daughter of Mussasa, was an Angolan Amazon, who was said to have one fierce eye (17th century).

The Heraean festival, held every four years in honor of the goddess Hera, included races for young unmarried women. The races were probably based on prior local sports events. The women ran in a short chiton, with loose hair and the left breast and shoulder bare. According to legend, Chloris was the first woman to win. Earlier reports of women athletes include the Minoan gymnasts who somersaulted over bulls and women wrestlers who engaged in mixed wrestling (!) on the island of Chios and Sparta (c. 8th century B.C.).

Alpheios and Kladeos are rivers surrounding the Olympian plain.

An unusual artist at the First Annual Women's Festival of the Arts at San Diego State College (now University) photographed herself – nude? in a body suit? – twisting head first down a tree. She made it into a wonderful poster that I cannot find.

COMMENTS

[From the Foreword to *Year of the Fires*, CWSS, 1983] What is mirrored in her poems is a is a breadth and generosity of spirit that is clear, active and knowable. And how refreshing it is, after reading the collection, to be in touch with a woman wrestling with themes including but not limited by uterine concerns….also in evidence is a musical ear delicately tuned to the melodies of a sensual earth. … a collection of poetry that matters.

Colette Inez, Poet, Memoirist, author of *Alive and Taking Name*

—✐—

Poet, teacher, traveler Joyce Nower presents a new book [(*Qin Warriors and Other Poems*, 2003] in three sections, each handsomely illustrated with an appropriate selection from classical artworks. The poems themselves speak with a poetic voice delicately attuned to the specific places they celebrate….A vast and profound scholarship peeks through in almost every poem…the photo at the back of her previous book, *Column of Silence* [is an] apt image for such a commanding voice. It shows her garbed in a Tae Kwon Do uniform, black belt and all, fists up and an expression as challenging as the mind behind her words. Feminist and humanist, here speaks a poet who has not merely observed the human condition in all its manifold guises, but has obviously internalized the many roles she studies. This voice… has the capacity to transport the reader almost virtually to the scene whereof it speaks. More information (including that great photo of the poet in martial getup) and more poems can be located at Nower's web site: joycenower.com

Sandy McKinney, Poet, author of *Body Grief*, **and translator of Spanish poet Rafael Guillen's** *I'm Speaking*

—✐—

A sharp and haunting connection between past and present… the relics of an ancient culture that still… impacts others even worlds away… The poetry in this 53 page collection [*Qin Warriors & Other Poems*, 2003] has the depth and vision and power of a poet in her prime. It is rare and almost perfect to come away from reading a volume of poetry with a feeling both of discovery and loss, knowing in it's completeness, our own inescapable end; and the realization that we too will darken into eternity but for the small temporary chance of light through inspired words. Some books, you pass on; I recommend this as a book you will keep in your library for a second and third read. You'll have to buy another copy for the friend.

Tikvah Feinstein, Editor of *Taproot Literary Review*

.——✍᠆——.

Your poems [*Year of the Fires*] are by my bed. At five I usually start the day with poems and this morning read Requiem – and found it very moving and startlingly original with its undertone of the theological Requiem we all know and which reverberates in a special way through the overtones of this one martyr's life. I Move Towards Stillness spoke to me very poignantly also. You are such a good poet. Thank you for sending me this treasure.

May Sarton (1912-1995) , Poet, author of *Collected Poems, 1930-1973*

Joyce Nower is the author of three other books of poetry, and her poems and articles have appeared in numerous journals. She has been the recipient of four successive Artists-in- Communities Awards from the California Arts Council, and has been nominated for a Pushcart Prize. During June of 1999, she gave lectures on contemporary American poetry at Sichuan Normal University, Shaanxi Normal University, and Yanan University in the People's Republic of China. She also wrote a poetry column called "Intersections" for the online magazine The Alsop Review. Joyce, a Third Degree Black Belt in Taekwondo, has an article entitled "Martial Arts and Feminist Awareness" in the November-December, 2009, issue of Off Our Backs. She lived with her family in La Mesa, California.